SIXTY-FOUR DAYS
OF A NORMANDY SUMMER

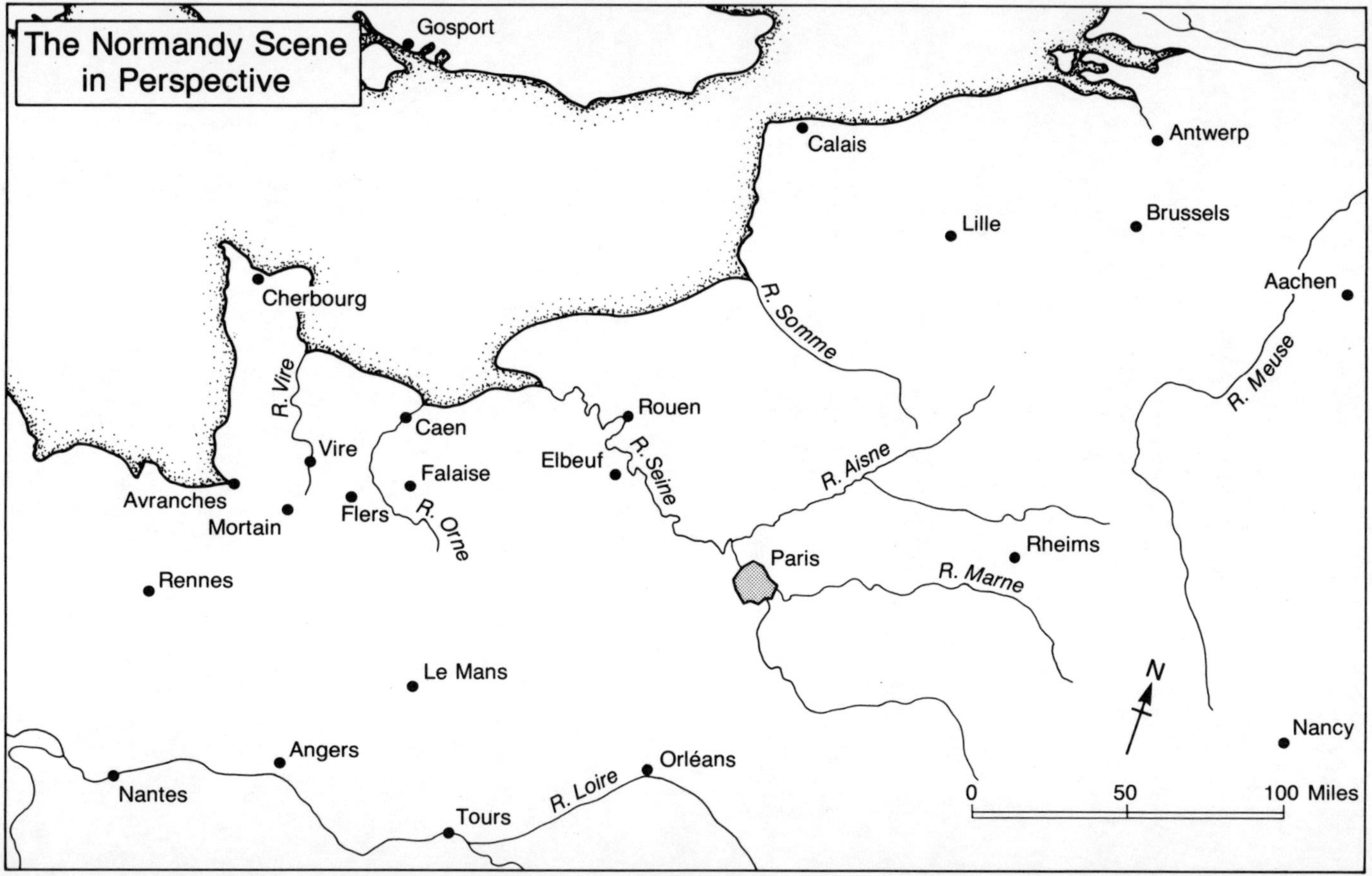
The Normandy Scene in Perspective
Gosport
Calais
Antwerp
Lille
Brussels
Aachen
Cherbourg
R. Somme
R. Meuse
R. Vire
Rouen
Caen
Vire
Elbeuf
Falaise
R. Seine
R. Aisne
Avranches
Flers
Mortain
R. Orne
Rheims
Paris
R. Marne
Rennes
Le Mans
N
Nancy
Angers
Orléans
Nantes
R. Loire
0
50
100 Miles
Tours

SIXTY-FOUR DAYS OF A NORMANDY SUMMER

With a Tank Unit after D-Day

KEITH JONES

ROBERT HALE · LONDON

First published in Great Britain 1990

Robert Hale Limited
Clerkenwell House
Clerkenwell Green
London EC1R 0HT

ISBN 0 7090 4240 X

Photoset in North Wales by
Derek Doyle & Associates, Mold, Clwyd.
Printed in Great Britain by
St Edmundsbury Press, Bury St Edmunds, Suffolk.
Bound by WBC Bookbinders.

Contents

Illustrations

Between pages 96 and 97

All pictures courtesy of the Imperial War Museum, London.

To my wife

Maps

Map artwork by Barking Dog Art.

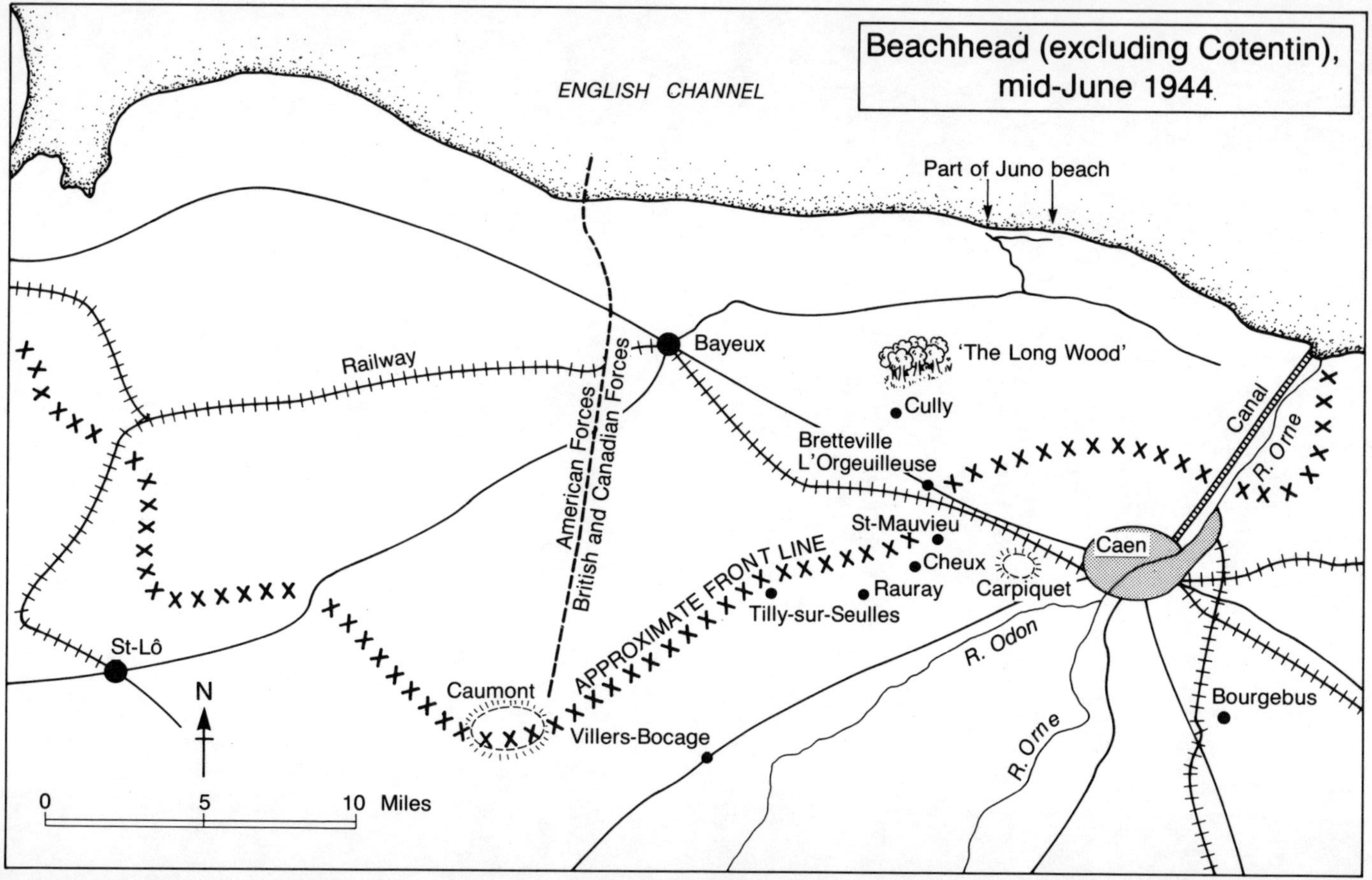
Beachhead (excluding Cotentin), mid-June 1944
ENGLISH CHANNEL
Part of Juno beach
Bayeux
'The Long Wood'
Cully
Railway
American Forces
British and Canadian Forces
Bretteville L'Orgeuilleuse
Canal
R. Orne
St-Mauvieu
Cheux
Caen
Carpiquet
Rauray
Tilly-sur-Seulles
APPROXIMATE FRONT LINE
R. Odon
St-Lô
N
Caumont
Villers-Bocage
Bourgebus
R. Orne
0
5
10
Miles

1 The Long Wood

The coastline was sighted below a haze about lunch-time on 14 June. After an hour it was scarcely clearer. The ship had hove to, would not stand in for the beach until some state of tide after dark. A group of us on deck surveyed the distant silence of the shore across an intervening calm of Channel.

It had been calm all the way from Gosport, where sun glinted on the wavelets during embarkation the day before. After an evening meal shared with our immaculately laundered hosts in their cramped wardroom, we took an after-dark peep from the deck, to contrast the hundred navigation lights moving around us with five years of land-bound black-out. In dimly lit quarters we put our inflatable 'horsecollars' handy, with the bags vomit* which no one was to need. Before attempting sleep, the padre and I separately began what was to prove an unremitting chore, censoring letters home.

Now, in daylight, we peered at what seemed a mile or two of blurred inactivity on land ahead. An occasional silent beach explosion sent a column of debris and dust vertically skyward. Residual mine detonation or long-range harassing fire? The group argued. Otherwise nothing to see. What had become of the invasion force that landed here eight days before us?

Waterproofed to above tank periscope level and under radio silence, we heard only at meal-times the bland naval

* In accordance with army vernacular, all equipment, small or large, was listed name-first followed by description.

version of continuing progress. In the Hampshire cages before embarkation the loudspeakers had played music-while-you-work, especially 'Little Lambs Eat Ivy', but as we quit the camp, was that not a *Daily Mirror* smuggled in and left lying about, with a picture of the shadow cast on an English haystack by the first pilotless buzzbomb? The liberation of Europe had begun but civilians in Britain had a new 'blitz' to experience.

The landing ship tank (LST) stood in at dusk but near the beach became grounded on a shoal or underwater tangle. Waiting on deck most of the short June night, while the Allied flak went up at Goering's succession of beach intruders, before tinkling down on deck all round us, our eyes adjusted to the dark. By the time the bow doors could be opened and the ramp lowered, it was near dawn on the 15th and there were only a few inches of sea left to wade through. Even in the gloom the shore felt and smelled like the seaside.

Then the scoutcar with a stranger driving it was taking me up some part of Juno Beach in the wake of the tanks of A Squadron and RHQ. Clear of the exit, our journey zigzagged on country roads. When we harboured in the long wood five miles inland, it was already day.

From among the trees 'Nobby' Clark, the car's usual driver, emerged to guide us into a space. He had been commandeered for advance party by the second-in-command, Lord George Scott, who had left me his driver. Now he placed two steaming mugs of tea on the engine cover, knocked on the waterproofing of the front vizor and gestured for the stranger to emerge. He cocked an eye at me, extricating my five-foot-eleven from the rigid canvas canopy rigged to enable a wade some two feet above the armoured hatch.

'Thought you must be sunk!'

'Stuck on a shoal. Bow doors jammed. I thought we might still be there for the next spring tides. Good lot the Navy though, offered for us to remember the LST number any time we want to desert.'

'What was the number?'

'Can't remember now.'

I was down on the ground, reaching for the tea. The 2 I/C's driver wriggled out of the same sole exit.

'Must be a bit claustrophobic in the front seat just now.'

I wanted to part amicably. He said nothing. His driving performance at embarkation and my irritation about it had not endeared us to each other. Nobby thrust the other mug into his hand and pointed where he should go to regain his usual vehicle.

'The sooner I get this wading muck off the better.'

Nobby's own vehicle was his joy. 'We shan't want it any more.' He pointed out the slit trench he had dug. 'Jerry patrols were chucking egg grenades just over that way the first night we got here. C Squadron has moved in there this morning.'

'Seems quiet enough since the tanks killed their engines. You'd think the war was miles away.'

'Oh it's moved back a bit since then; must have known the regiment was coming.'

It was sometimes difficult to know when Nobby was being serious. With the yeomen since embodiment in '39, he had seen 'a few' changes prior to the unit leaving Britain, and had earned his one stripe: probably the best Humber scoutcar driver in the regiment, according to Edward Fletcher, the recce troop leader. By contrast I had joined them less than a year ago, from a Royal West Kent lorried infantry battalion converted to armoured cars, trained for a year and disbanded.

I sought out the adjutant, Robert Lorimer. He was as usual talking aloud to Alastair Hetherington, the intelligence officer.

'Oh good, here's Keith,' said Bobby. 'Look, we're all expected to keep out of sight in this minor forest. But you as regimental liaison officer will be able to get out and about and find your way around, ready to meet the other formations we're going to work with in the first action – that's when they arrive. Meanwhile you'll be able to make the acquaintance of the natives, pick up some butter and cheese for the mess, practise your French, if that's what they speak in Normandy.'

Alastair and I exchanged glances. We knew our Bobby, or thought we did.

'Each afternoon the whole unit will bed down for compulsory rest.' It sounded just like some of the exercises we had taken part in in Britain. 'But not Keith!'

All the same, I managed a good sleep on that, the unit's first day of active service overseas. I have always liked my sleep.

My first excursion was to map-read Nobby to the dentist. He drove us to some neat brown tents on a cliff overlooking the now slightly choppy Channel. While Nobby reported for torture and relief, I relaxed, enjoying the sea air, my gaze wandering idly round the medical encampment, day-dreaming. A vision emerged from a bell-tent, unmistakably, outstandingly female. I watched in silence. The khaki figure moved lithely from tent to small marquee and vanished. I was still looking when a voice spoke from behind my left shoulder.

'Yes, we have a dozen of them. Been here since the beginning. I can see that surprises you.'

I turned to see a medical full colonel smiling affably.

When Nobby returned for the drive back, he was slow to believe my anecdote, his problem having been dealt with entirely by men.

The regiment's long wood was pleasantly quiet. Pigeon flew between the trees from the grass on one side to the crops on the other. Crows flapped overhead, uttering the same cries as their brothers in Britain. Flies were not obtrusive. The sky showed through gaps in the foliage, summer clouds varying the sun's patterning of branch and leaf upon the bivouac sheets draped from vehicles to turf and on protruding groundsheets and blankets, which wrapped each afternoon of compulsory rest. Whatever cliché you use about the calm before the storm, there is something about an environment of deciduous trees. A police chief once expressed it in three words of his native language: '*Das beruhigt mich*!' – 'It soothes me!' The serenity of the long wood could not have failed to affect the regiment, and for me, who had less of it than they, it would abide to the end.

A bumpy track ran the length of our cover. Along it once a day each way a farm labourer rode his bicycle, always at eyes front below his tight blue beret, as if we and our forty-two Cromwell tanks (only two squadrons and RHQ) and other wagons were not there. My imagination worked on what his real purpose and identity might be – he clearly was not selling onions – but I soon had other things to do.

The official purpose of my visits to units with which we should be working was to find out for my colonel who was who, what they looked like, how they were equipped and how they worked; conversely to show them what battledress badges and flashes we wore, and tell them what our new British Cromwell tanks looked like, there being no photographs or drawings available.

So in the next week, accompanied by a second LO, Ernie Ehrenfeld, I made the acquaintance, in green and unspoiled countryside, of two regiments and the HQ of 31st Tank Brigade, then of three regiments, the motor battalion, gunners and HQ of the independent 4th Armoured Brigade. There at the County of London Yeomanry I enquired after Geoffrey Brook, whom I had last seen four or five years ago as a recently embodied Territorial lance-corporal before they went off to Egypt. Yes, they said now, in the CO's tank!

I clambered up the Sherman, knocking politely on the turret top. Sergeant Geoff looked up at me in mild surprise. He was his colonel's radio-operator.

'I thought you wanted the infantry, young Keith!'

'I got it. My battalion was converted to Royal Armoured Corps. I expected you to have a commission long since.'

'I could have, but a unit like this grows on you.'

At 4th Armoured HQ with its sign of the Black Jerboa, Brigadier John Currie gave us tea with tinned jam and rich Normandy butter on fresh ration bread. The sun shone. Someone made a remark about it being singular for an artilleryman to command armour. Our host responded in a way I was to remember.

'Whenever I'm succeeded in this command, I have no doubt it will be by a black beret.'

I presumed he meant someone from the Royal Tank Regiment. His words were to be prophetic, and very soon.

The other formation to see was 15th Scottish, an infantry division as fresh from Britain and untried as our own. There were nine battalions in three brigades plus their support companies to meet. Some of the Jocks were late arriving, owing to the storm that carried away the American mulberry,* severely damaged the British one, stranded 800 craft up the beaches and generally played havoc with the troop and supply build-up for days following 19 June. In one of the brigades many people were still green from their hours of sea-sickness, but everyone was generous in paying attention to Ernie and me on our well-intentioned mission.

Whether out on visits or back in the wood, we heard little or no noise of battle. Although five miles inland, we were all of three miles from the nearest part of the front line, to establish which most major thrusts had been made before our arrival. Distance prevented our hearing the Americans fighting to reach the west coast of Normandy by the 18th, hold their southern boundary and move north on Cherbourg.

It was Alastair's visits to division that brought to a few of us one version of what happened to a British armoured push in the forty-eight hours before we landed. Cromwell tanks in the leading regiment of 7th Armoured Division – the Desert Rats brought home from Italy last Christmas and landed on D + 1 – had penetrated close-wooded country to Villers-Bocage, over five miles south of where the enemy was still hanging on to Tilly-sur-Seulles. The column was line ahead in the main street when Tiger tanks suddenly appeared from among the trees and knocked out one Cromwell after another at point-blank range. The British crews had watched their own 75 mm shots bouncing harmlessly off the frontal and turret

* Service code-name for the pre-fabricated harbour structure which enabled landing of materials at most states of tide on a sloping beach.

armour of the Tigers. In face of mounting casualties, the famous Rats had been pulled back, so the story went. The impact of this tale about the effect of German 88 mm gunnery on our fast-moving cruiser just making its début in Normandy can be imagined.

I joined a small group making an afternoon visit to the front line in the Canadian sector, where our corps attack would begin. If any of the group had expected to see any kind of line – ours or the enemy's, they were to be disappointed. Each side was at pains to conceal its positions, which probably kept changing. Even the patrolled intervening no man's land was of indeterminate area, varying, fluid. As a trained but untried infantier, I found it fascinating that I failed to spot even one of the Canadian forward positions or outposts. Their guide was careful not to take us near any. Nor did he mention the scale and ferocity of the SS attack they had sustained a fortnight before, holding their ground in spite of their losses. He did point out one Panther tank (forty-five tons) drooping its long, high-velocity gun at the main Caen–Bayeux road, where the monster had been knocked out by an infantry Piat* at very close Canadian range.

As I got back to the wood, the MO and an orderly were just moving off in a jeep towards C Squadron.

'Near the end of compulsory rest we heard a solitary shot, something like a Sten or a Schmeisser.' Bobby Lorimer, the adjutant related how he had dressed quickly and stepped out to intercept C Squadron sergeant-major in the jeep, come to collect the MO. A troop leader had been shot in the leg, while he rested. Was this a battle accident, a self-inflicted wound or a sniper? Tim Peck, the squadron commander, had asked his subaltern, who seemed barely awake. Ruefully holding the wounded limb and its oozing purple spot that would be his ticket to the UK, he favoured the sniper theory. A scouring party had been organized, but three miles was some way for a sniper

* Portable close-range anti-tank weapon carried by British and Canadian infantry.

to penetrate, and some wags were already speculating how much a neighbouring unit of medium artillery knew about handling its small arms.

After dinner Alastair and I took a stroll in the general direction of the landing beaches. I commented on the absence from the meal of Edward Fletcher of the recce troop, the badges of whose service dress were of a Hussar regiment not brought home for this campaign. All winter in Yorkshire Edward had entertained the subalterns' mess with a repertoire of stories that had us creased with laughter, and bawdy songs in which everyone joined.

'We can't make a noise like that here.' Alastair was serious about it. 'Besides, Edward seems resolved upon spending all his time up on one or another sector of the front line with his binoculars, seeing what he can see of the enemy. Getting ready to excel at his reconnaissance role, I suppose.'

'He'll need to do better than I did this afternoon. Didn't see a living soul of either side.'

As we walked I reflected that our regiment's recce troop was all Daimler scoutcars, whereas the armoured regiments had some Honey tanks. The June light was at last beginning to fade when we came upon a Sherman Firefly tank standing alone on short grass beside a small copse. The long seventeen-pounder gun kept guard against the evening sky but the tank was deserted, silent. The two of us had studied samples of this Anglo-American innovation on our pre-breakfast jogs around Aldershot last month. Armoured regiments had Fireflies on a basis of one tank in four, the British seventeen-pounder built to penetrate Tiger and Panther frontal armour. Our own unit, as divisional armoured reconnaissance, had no Fireflies.

We took in that this abandoned model sported the latest reinforced armour on its front apron. Then Alastair found the 88 mm hole in it at the thickest part, and I nearly fell over the three white crosses in a darkening earth patch beside the vehicle. Each was painted in black with a name, rank and number: a second lieutenant, lance-corporal and trooper of 4th/7th Dragoon Guards, an assault regiment. How silent, how peaceful was this, their first resting-place! Three out of five crew: I wondered, was that a usual pattern?

The night had become cooler. We turned back for the long wood. Before we could regain it, darkness would be complete. Most of the way we were silent, thinking. Alastair wanted to survive to become a great editor, I to experience living with my young wife. Probably everyone else wanted to survive too, including the enemy. When Alastair spoke, he sounded almost angry. I felt he was camouflaging his true emotions in an apparently tough criticism of practice.

'That tank must have stood there for over two weeks. It should have been recovered by now. Especially a Firefly! The Germans would have done it next day, or same night.'

I thought of the Panther that had stood unclaimed for nearly as long in the sector I had just visited. I said nothing. The Panther was in no man's land, within Canadian surveillance.

Next evening I departed to liaise with the division's armoured brigade. The attack was to begin the morning after that, 26 June. Because of the storm and the American pace of progress, it would be starting eight days later than General Montgomery had intended. When it moved out on the morrow, the regiment had spent eleven days in the long wood.

Of Alastair's story from division about the Cromwell tank's 'blooding' at Villers-Bocage, fuller versions were later to be learned. It seems undoubted that the armoured brigade commander, 'Loony' Hinde, had regained control of Villers by late afternoon, beating off further attacks in which Panzer Lehr lost several Mark IV tanks and six of its 'under command' Tiger unit. More defensible than the town for a force short of infantry was some nearby high ground, to which the brigadier withdrew his command for the night and where next day it demolished a savage assault in which grenadiers of the veteran 2nd Panzer Division – newly arrived from Amiens – also took part.

Withdrawing the 7th was a corps decision; the loss in Cromwells, some twenty-seven.

2 First Graze

After dinner on 25 June Robert and Alastair saw me off. Lance-Corporal Nobby Clark had the scoutcar stowed and ready. I mounted up, sat on the back roof, legs dangling into the hatchway, map board resting against the Bren gun clamped across the hull top. We bumped our way along the track out of the long wood onto another country road. It led over a slight spur and down the other side to the village of Cully, location of the armoured brigade HQ.

The short trip was entirely relaxed, in keeping with a mild and dry June evening, pistol ports open to give the driver air. Near the highest point an incredibly old woman was trying to extract water from an even older pump. I drew Nobby's attention to her but he had been watching the road and she was already beyond his visual arc. We did not know then that six miles further south during the day a heavy and persistent mist had prevented the 49th Infantry Division from capturing Rauray, a piece of high ground to the right of our stated boundary for the morrow, from which the enemy would therefore overlook the entire corps operation and bring fire to bear on it. Similar murky weather over airfields in southern England was about to mean no air support during the first two days of the operation.

At Cully we were directed to Tac Brigade,* where their several liaison officers welcomed us into the orchard, enthused about the weight of artillery located all round,

* A formation commander's immediate 'tactical' escort at the front – where it would be impractical to take Main HQ.

the high morale of the armoured regiments, comprehensiveness of the wall map in the armoured command vehicle (ACV) at Main Brigade, which I must see in the daylight of next morning. It was becoming dusk as we were appointed to break rations with a Sherman crew, seven of us to the standard fourteen-man pack. We rigged the bivouac sheet on one side of the Humber. I decided to sleep in pyjamas and turned in.

During most of its three years training in Britain, the brigade had comprised two cavalry and one yeomanry units besides its motorized infantry battalion, but early in 1944 one cavalry regiment left for an independent brigade and was replaced by a Royal Tank Regiment, serious professionals who had defended Calais in 1940 and been in Greece in 1941 and at Gazala in 1942, then attacked from Alamein to Tunis and beyond. How much their personnel had changed during that awesome record I should never know, but everyone could be confident they retained a hard core of very battle-experienced people.

The guns woke me at barely first light. Seemingly every artillery piece for miles was ranging on the morning targets, but it was the field battery in the orchard separated from us only by a hedge and farm track which made sure I was aroused. I got up and dressed, rolled my blanket, found my safety razor and some cold water, checked the time, switched on the car radio to warm. The tarpaulin surface and surrounding foliage implied some wetness in the night, perhaps heavy dew. Only later did we hear that scarcely three miles away the Scottish division on its start line had been thoroughly wetted by heavy rain.

Nobby was still hidden under the bivouac when the netting call* from regiment back in the long wood came through. I checked the net and answered up in my turn, strength five. Nobby's netting yesterday was proved

* A daily check of the network by command radio saw that all outstations were accurately tuned in.

spot-on, the distance and terrain separating us from RHQ insufficient to mar reception. Of the rest of the net, I heard the rear link tanks of the two squadrons answering, the recce troop, A echelon and some others that I recognized above the gun noise. I knew that Ernie Ehrenfeld was not being detached for liaison duty at present.

Suddenly the gunners finished ranging. Before I recovered from the silence, Nobby surfaced, pulling on his trousers over the shirt he had slept in.

'The regiment's all right then.'

In no time at all he had the petrol cooker working and a tin of sausages heating for breakfast, as well as water to supply a day's tea into mugs and the several thermos flasks the car carried. Nobby had prepared for this war when kitting out our chariot back in Aldershot. He had even scrounged from the fitters two spare sheets of armour plating to slide under each seat, to minimize our injuries if the car should go up on a mine.

With the guns silent we could hear one or two comings-and-goings above the hissing of the field battery's cookers, a jeep that drove up to the brigadier's tank, a dispatch rider who moved off, roared through the lane between the orchards and disappeared up the rise in the direction of Divisional HQ. There was no rush for 11th Armoured to move down because the Scotsmen had to make their initial assault and leave some space for the armour to assemble in.

We had eaten and attended to other needs when the brigadier himself looked by to acknowledge my purpose in being there, asking hospitably if we had breakfasted and then if I'd seen any sign of the RAF liaison officer yet. The brigade was to have rocket-firing Typhoons on call, weather permitting. There was no sun yet and a fair amount of cloud about when the artillery started up again, not just our locals but medium and heavy guns and – we were assured even if we could not definitely identify – the Royal Navy's big stuff from just off shore. The invisible defenders of St-Mauvieu and Cheux, or the positions they were thought to be occupying, were the recipients of this overkill by high explosive.

When Tac Brigade moved out, Nobby followed our rations Sherman, which was only a few vehicles behind the brigadier's. Like so many military exercises in Britain, this was full of stop and start and 'There's old so-and-so', with everyone trying to look casual. For the Scotsmen assaulting the heights we could not yet see, and for the crews of the lumbering Churchill tanks supporting them, the pace must have felt much more urgent.

During one of the many halts a rifleman from the motor battalion came up to the scoutcar, carrying his Bren gun, which looked too big for his five-foot-five height and slight build. The moment his breezy grin was beamed at me, I recognized him as Donald Gillate, from our time at school, or rather out of school because he was a year behind me and our paths seldom crossed in school. We had sometimes found ourselves on the same train homeward, after which he had further to walk from the station than I did. He had always seemed full of bright chatter, likeable.

'I thought it was you. Is there room in there for me if things get too hot?'

His casual greeting came just as if eight years had not intervened. At his use of the word 'hot', I remembered something he had related about an early girlfriend, who must have been all of fifteen: that he had given her up because she was not 'hot enough'. Now he must be joking about getting inside the scoutcar. Edward, Nobby and I had made a driving practice trip in it six weeks ago but one of us always had to be on the engine cover.

'Not a chance, Donald. Take a look!'

The column moved off. With a nonchalant wave of his free hand to acknowledge my injunction to look me up again when he could, Donald vanished back into the bushes.

Tac Brigade took an age to reach Bretteville and the knocked-out Panther. Then we crossed the Caen–Bayeux railway and the HQ halted on the left while the Sherman regiments came through to deploy into open country.

Some press correspondents arrived in a jeep and saw the GSO 3 (captain) in the lee of the command tank.

The Scotsmen had disappeared up the expanse of cornfields and over the first crest. It was from somewhere beyond it that thick black smoke was rising steadily, from the target that was Cheux village on its ridge. The leading Jock brigades had reached their objectives by nine o'clock but the Tank Brigade Churchills had been held up by minefields, and also had to engage enemy tanks which fired on them before retiring south of the Scots' objectives. Now, it was said, the rubble and fires of Cheux were obstructing tank passage through it. Any formation finding a way beyond the village experienced withering fire of all kinds from the next enemy defence network, which included tanks of the 12th SS Panzer Division in strength. No one told us – perhaps it was not known then – that the formation had shot more than a score of its Canadian prisoners since D-Day.

The corps plan had been that, as soon as the Scots were established in Cheux, one squadron of my regiment would exploit through to reach the River Odon, nearly three miles beyond. If successful, its path would be used for the entire armoured brigade. Instead of the squadron's being called forward soon after nine o'clock, it was now well beyond noon when I heard sounds of activity on our previously silent radio. The brigadier led his Tac HQ higher up the slope, signalling me to go over and report.

Leaving Nobby monitoring the regimental net, I dismounted, went over to the Sherman with the wooden gun, climbed up to stand behind the turret with my map board. The brigadier removed his headphones, enquired if my squadron had reached its assembly area, asked me to keep him current on progress.

When I reached the Humber again, A Squadron commander was on the net, telling our colonel that 'Big Sunray' had just joined him on the start line. I inferred that the squadron was at last through Cheux and was being launched by the divisional commander in person. I also sensed my colonel's irritation at his own delay and failure to reach the rendezvous before the general.

From then on, it was the voice of the squadron's rear link captain, sometimes only in belated response to the colonel's persistent questioning, which brought an occasional bulletin to Nobby and me of the twenty tanks now probing into the unknown. Nobby passed me some buttered biscuit and bully-beef he had prepared. We settled down to eat and listen.

Two enemy shells burst one by one, straddling Tac Brigade. The press concluded their parley with the G3 (captain), who mounted the turret to rejoin his brigadier. Having learned nothing more than Div. HQ had told them earlier that morning, they now drove off in their exposed jeep to report a slow-moving battle. The sunshine became noticeably hot.

The yeomanry practice of having a separate radio net for each squadron had the disadvantage that the only information reaching the colonel on regimental net was the squadron rear link captain's impression of what was happening. If the squadron commander was too preoccupied to pass to his captain snippets of 'picture' from time to time over the short-range 'B' set, the captain's information, denied a chance to listen in to squadron net by the requirement to stay tuned to the regimental one, could be quite limited.

As Nobby and I munched and listened now, I pictured the captain, a civilian-life solicitor who in barracks used to take off his wristwatch each morning to time himself over breakfast, and wondered wickedly to myself during a long silence whether he had been timing the squadron over its start-line. Pressed by the colonel to say something, he summarized that they were deployed in a kind of long meadow hemmed in by hedgerows, from which they were being sniped at and mortared on all sides. Grenades were being lobbed onto vehicles near the perimeter. The AA tank (twin 20 mm Oerlikons turreted on a cruiser hull) was strafing the hedgerows.

'MG traverse right, 300.'

The fire order was repeated urgently before the legal

mind remembered he was on 'A' set. It was as he switched to 'intercom' that a next question came from his colonel, not heard, so unanswered. In the body of the scoutcar I could see Nobby sitting bolt upright to catch what was happening to his mates in the squadron. When the captain next switched to 'A' set, it was to report a cruiser tank hit.

I walked across to report to the brigadier. As I returned, the RAF half-track arrived from the direction of the railway line, coming to a halt near the Humber. (For me the RAF is eternally associated with my great friend John Lockhart, who flew Hurricanes and had been posted 'missing' since March.) I waited hospitably to greet the flight lieutenant and point out the brig's tank before climbing back into the car. Nobby said our armoured squadron seemed stuck; nothing fresh since I left.

As I put on the headphones, our colonel's impatience, unlike Nobby's, which had to be endured, broke out in a new demand for situation report. Rear link said it was a Sunray minor (troop leader) vehicle hit. Some crew had baled out into the long grass. The 'meadow' was crawling alive with bazooka men.

The colonel wanted to know when he was going to hear what the squadron was doing! A long silence could have meant that the captain was pressing his squadron commander on 'B' set for 'picture'. Switching back, he told the colonel they were probing on. In the hiatus that followed, I noticed that the RAF LO was leaning on the Humber listening to the commentary as if it were ice hockey or the boat race. We exchanged grins. I handed him one of Nobby's bully biscuit butties. He made a face but began gnawing it mechanically.

The captain announced that the squadron's two 95 mm guns were giving supporting fire. One troop had almost reached the far end. Nobby knew that the close-support tanks were manned by the squadron HQ sergeant and the captain 2 I/C, both regimental gunnery experts. I imagined the two range masters using their binoculars just above turret rim, concentrating on blasting the distant target to powder. Outside the scoutcar, one of the brigade LOs was listening, next to the flight lieutenant. Two more enemy shells landed nearby but neither listener moved.

The next rear-link broadcast said the leading troop reported a twelve-foot ditch beyond the far hedge. The colonel at once asked if they were putting a vehicle across it. He waited five minutes before he pressed for an answer.

'Just a minute, Colonel. Wyvil's been sniped!'

'Who?' In his scoutcar the CO had not quite heard.

From way back at the colonel's command truck, the adjutant's voice disciplined the net: 'Do not mention names and ranks on the air! Out!!'

The outside listeners chortled; not so Nobby, who was gripping the Humber's large horizontal steering-wheel.

The next silence was ended at last by that rustling noise on the net which denotes someone has pressed the prestle-switch on his microphone ready to transmit. The sound was irritatingly prolonged because no one spoke. But while the noise continued, no one else could speak and be heard. This included the CO.

When the squadron commander's voice came through, I thought it quite unlike his usual tone. Nobby said aloud: 'Major Peel.'

'Are you with Big Sunray? Over.'

Surprised as he may have been by the question, the colonel had caught up with his general. He acknowledged.

'Look, I've seen the ditch.' The major breathed hard. 'It's a sheer drop. We can't cross it. This field is the same on three sides.'

The major paused for his 'no through way' message to sink in. He sounded choked that, of all the impossible avenues for exploiting through to the river, this one had been chosen for him. We should many of us learn soon enough how frequently fields at least as baffling to tank progress could occur in traditional patterns of the Norman agriculture. For the moment, we listened for more.

'I've lost two cruisers. My second in command is dead. I want to come back. Over.'

At last he released the switch. The net was free for someone else to speak. No one did. I forced myself to go over to the command tank and report. If the agile Cromwell could not get further than the end of the field without capsizing, how could the taller Sherman? The brigade would have to try another route.

When I got back, Nobby still seemed stunned by the news of our first casualties. The RAF and the brigade LOs were listening for what might happen next. The rear link captain gave another fire order on 'A' set, switched to 'intercom' to repeat it, came back to regimental net to emphasize the squadron's plight. They were hemmed in. Things were getting hotter. They were sitting ducks. He was waiting, waiting, waiting for orders to pull back.

Nobby started the engine. Brigade was moving. The other listeners dived for their vehicles, the RAF LO shouting he would follow me. Nobby let in the clutch. We were behind our usual Sherman, rolling through the corn which gleamed each side of the lanes where tracks and wheels had laid it flat, over the rise to begin a gradual descent on the far side. I listened to the radio, looking at my map and thinking about the position of the squadron over a mile in front of us, listened until the order to withdraw to assembly area was sent out to the waiting rear link captain.

A shape in the trampled corn caught my attention, a field-grey uniform out of which had burst a prodigious tangle of intestine. Then we were beyond it.

'Did you see that, Nobby?'

I spoke to him on intercom but he was concentrating on 'A' set, listening for news of the squadron's other casualties. Another corpse came briefly into view close to our way, a major in the darker-toned Canadian battledress, a black powderburn surrounding the hole in his temple. He must have been there since a night patrol in what had been no man's land until today.

As the scoutcar approached an extensive copse at the foot of the valley, the Sherman commander in front turned to wave palm downwards at me before withdrawing into his turret hatch. I made a similar sign to the RAF half-track following us, then moved the lever to shift my seat to its lower position, which brought most of my head below roof-level. Presumably the copse had not been cleared. I reached forward to close the pistol port nearest to Nobby's head.

Some distance up the next slope vehicle commanders were emerging above hatches again and the column halted. The corn had been left behind, replaced by short grass. In the bright sunlight, there were the A Squadron Cromwells newly withdrawn and still line astern facing the beaches, but halted to allow crews to recuperate. Spotting Major Peel, I dismounted and walked over to where he stood aside from his tank, plucking at his multicoloured neckerchief, waiting for the colonel.

'Wyvil got it between the eyes,' he told me of his late second in command. 'Must have died at once.'

I asked about the crews who had baled out. Two were back and he hoped more would come later. He knew the names of each one missing, killed or wounded. I sensed his grief, edged with self-reproach. He had lost men for whom he was responsible. It did not consciously occur to me then that his experience was in due course to be mine also. The strength of his suppressed emotion was evoking my useless response in sympathetic murmurs when the colonel arrived with the divisional commander. I retired to the scoutcar to tell Nobby what I had heard.

It was the G3 who told me a few minutes later about the change of plan. The Scottish reserve brigade would punch through to a further objective in the direction of the river. To do this they would be supported not only by the Tank Brigade Churchills but by the combined fire power of our own armoured brigade and of the 4th, now coming up.

No sooner had I heard the plan than it was happening. From way back, all the artillery started banging away at new targets. From all round, the Shermans of six armoured regiments fanned out towards the southern skyline to look for targets. Dark clouds now suddenly obscured the sun and dimmed the whole battlefield, highlighting the hostile black crackling airbursts above the Sherman turrets as they topped the far rise.

Tac Brigade moved to the floor of the valley to protect a conference of top brass – brigade, divisional and corps – for which Nobby and I could have had a front seat if we had turned the car or screwed our heads round.

On the valley floor, our attention moved to a fifteen hundredweight ammunition truck that collected a shell splinter and went on fire in our midst, bullets popping off and whipping all round. I lowered my seat, and Nobby closed left pistol ports before passing me a thermos flask. The tea I poured was beginning to cool and tasted distinctly of cork. The regimental net was silent. Nobby was buttering more biscuits. I rested my head on the back of the open hatch and dozed.

Some time later the divisional commander's new ADC, Charles Pidduck roused me. I had known him as an amiable Div. LO back in Aldershot. Now he grinned his recent promotion into the hatch at me, twitting me about hiding away from the firecrackers, now nearly spent. He confided that the Jocks were having a bad time in their push for the new objective, and their supporting Churchills a worse one.

'The Shermans are getting stuck in now. Perhaps they'll see the Scotties forward to the jolly old river line.'

'What will my regiment be doing, Charles?'

'They're having a rest just now. Bit of a basin full. Tomorrow perhaps, right flank protection?'

'That won't be a picnic. Has 49 Div. taken Rauray yet?'

I looked over to the right but foliage made the area inscrutable.

'We shall know tonight, I expect. Meanwhile what is of much more interest is what the old Boche can trot out of strategic reserve in time to tackle our little push. What are they trundling up from places like the South of France?'

'Or from the Eastern Front?'

'There are some seasoned units due back from the east, but they may be recalled because the Soviet summer offensive began two days ago.'

Charles spotted that his general was ready to go and excused himself: 'When this show is over, you must bring Alastair to tea.'

Walking back to the GOC's Cromwell that sported the divisional pennant, he mounted up and they were away. Watching the conclave break up, I recognized the commander 4th Armoured – my recent tea-time host – leaving. He was standing up in his scoutcar, which took him up the slope towards the skyline among his own Shermans. It was his attitude as much as his flat gunner's hat with its wide red band that made him conspicuous. When his scoutcar halted, he stood on the roof, his binoculars scanning the area beyond the crest. He was probably in much the same position later that afternoon when an airburst killed him.

The valley remained dry. Lowering skies above the ridge ahead loosed their water on friend and foe. The Shermans seemed not to be firing much. Were there no visible targets? Dusk came without obvious change. Tac Brigade moved back to the large copse, where Main had established itself along the fringe. Nobby and I found a space and bivouacked beside the Humber.

At the end of our first day in action, unlike some others we did not seem to have been in any real danger. Four years in the wartime Army, at the age of twenty-three I had today seen the first corpses in my whole life. Nobby and I were being broken in very gently to the realities of battle, at second-hand so far. This was also the day Cherbourg was surrendered to the Americans, but if we heard about it, then or next day, we did not much care. I again put on pyjamas, fell asleep at once.

3 Up the Hill

Tac HQ moved off smartly on the 27th. To tag along meant skipping some of our usual preparations, such as brewing a tea supply. The column drove half-way up the open slope and stopped. The Shermans had gone from the skyline, there was nothing to see or hear. When enemy shellbursts began to reach us in a desultory but menacing fashion, everyone stayed in his vehicle.

I had taken the morning call from regiment on the way up, but no traffic had come over the net since. No news of what the yeomen were doing was matched by no brief from the brigadier, who had sensibly withdrawn into his turret when the shelling began.

By elevenses I directed Nobby to take us back to Main Brigade at the copse, where we could catch up on the things we had left undone. I walked along to the ACV, where the IO gave me tea and all the information I lacked. Rauray had still not been captured, so continued to hold up our efforts on the right, probably also responsible for the shells currently falling around Tac HQ.

On the left the Scotsmen had struggled forward against the 12th SS before dark yesterday to the Colleville area and the railway line joining Caen with Villers-Bocage. They spent an uncomfortable and damp night there, for the rain had deluged on that side of the ridge. Some Shermans were trying to support them again today, but with turrets being sniped and in thick country where infantier and tankman were glad to use the available cover, communication was not straightforward. My regiment was

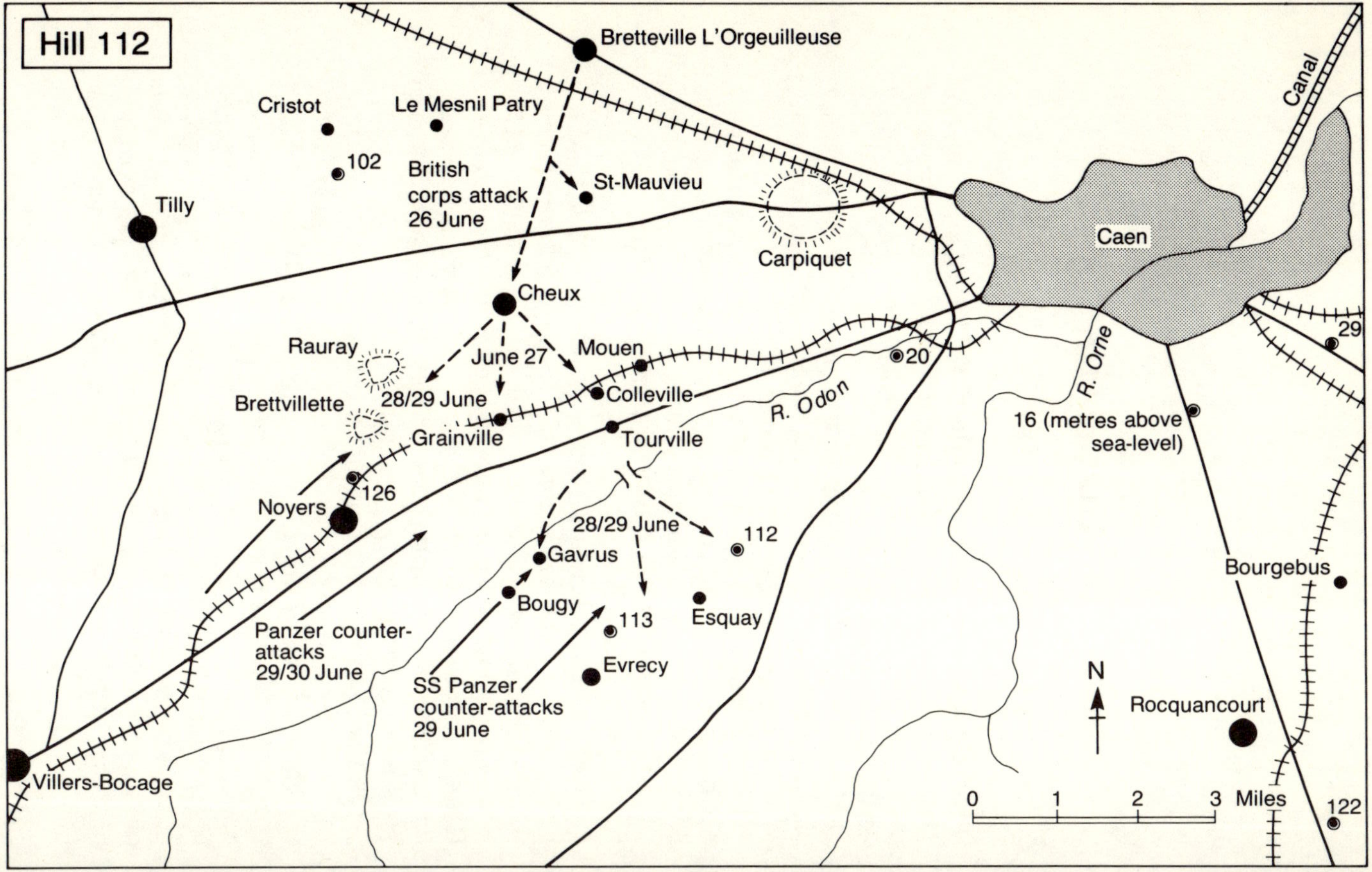

Hill 112
Bretteville L'Orgeuilleuse
Cristot
Le Mesnil Patry
102
British
corps attack
26 June
St-Mauvieu
Tilly
Carpiquet
Caen
Canal
Cheux
Rauray
June 27
Mouen
28/29 June
Colleville
Brettvillette
Grainville
Tourville
R. Odon
20
R. Orne
29
16 (metres above
sea-level)
126
Noyers
28/29 June
112
Gavrus
Bougy
113
Esquay
Bourgebus
Panzer counter-
attacks
29/30 June
SS Panzer
counter-attacks
29 June
Evrecy
N
Rocquancourt
Villers-Bocage
0
1
2
3
Miles
122

resting, with no role yet, but that could change at any moment.

I told Nobby about the regiment, then took the shovel into the copse to make myself comfortable clear of the Main Brigade area. It was an attractive scene, with dells and small hillocks as well as a clearing or two. Feeling better already, I walked another fifty yards in, spotted a slit trench on a rise, and in it a bare-headed German infantryman standing to against the British assault. I went up to him. His rifle was gone, his steel helmet on the ground just in front of him. Below a thatch of almost black hair his face and neck were weatherbeaten, green and copper, not grey as I would have expected. I could see no obvious wound, yet rigor mortis had confirmed his upright position in the trench. I murmured something about his war being over – like Wyvil Raynsford's, the first of many more to come.

Unhurriedly I regained the Humber, asked Nobby if all was ready for a return to Tac Brigade. Several bursts of Sten-gun fire sounded from the area I had just left. Moments later a sergeant with quite a squad of soldiers apparently protecting Main Brigade broke cover between our car and the ACV.

'What's to do, Sergeant?'

'Snipers, sir. We've just flushed the copse.'

Strapping the shovel back onto the car, I was thankful to have completed my business before the copse was flushed. I wondered if any of the Stens had put holes in the peace of my lone German sentinel. Why, if there had been any live snipers within range when I paid him my last respects, had they not shot at me?

We returned up the slope just as Tac HQ was moving off and in time to take our place behind the ration Sherman. Another tank followed behind us. There was no time to notice what had happened to the RAF half-track. The column moved up to the crest and over, approaching Cheux, from which smoke still rose.

A brigade LO drove back along the line of vehicles, warning each crew that the place harboured snipers.

Thinking that among buildings it was also easy to lob grenades, I slid the front hatch of the Humber closed over Nobby's head, unlatched and slammed home all pistol ports, while Nobby eased down his vizor to the bullet-proof glass block. I had stowed my map board, grabbed my steel helmet from the radio top and regained my seat, which I was about to lower, when I noticed that our wheels were awash in water as we bumped into the 'street' past the first grey stone building. I watched to see if the water was going to get any deeper, pondering what might have caused the flood (a damaged water tower or pump water used to fight the fires?), when a sudden swipe past my ear that stung the whole cheek reinforced the crack of a single shot. A neat round hole had appeared in the Bren-gun butt clamped in front of my head.

My thinking slowed to a snail's pace, questioning whether the hole had been there earlier. Unbelievingly I turned to see if some chump behind had accidentally loosed off a round. That act woke me up, because every vehicle in view was closed down tight. My own seat went down with a bump. I pulled the hatch to above my dreamy head, replacing the infantry-style steel helmet on the radio top as the car lurched on through the village.

Being closed down means not knowing what is happening outside. I opened my pistol port to see an armoured bulldozer clearing rubble to widen the intended corps axis. Beyond the last building I opened the hatch cover again as we passed several knocked-out Churchill tanks. Further on a silent Cromwell painted on turret side with a white triangle denoting A Squadron showed through a hedge where the adjoining field was above our level.

Tac Brigade had skirted the 'meadow' of yesterday's probe fiasco, and now halted at the far end of and below it. Hatches opened and crews emerged into dazzling sunshine. The official explanation of the Cheux flooding as produced by a recent cloudburst seemed difficult to credit.

Exploring the gulley surrounding the raised field,

Nobby and I moved from light into darkness, tripping over an enormous unburied defender still clutching a stick grenade, treading into a pile of human excrement. As our eyes adjusted, abandoned bazookas and cylindrical gas-mask containers showed up, but the fresh June air of five paces away was replaced by what everyone was soon complaining about daily as the sweet-and-sour stench of defecation and death.

'Major Peel done better than the Churchills.'

Nobby was reckoning in terms of casualties, and not of the extra mile of ground that the afternoon push had gained where A Squadron's attempt had failed. The forty-ton Churchills had thicker armour than the Cromwells, slowing them down to a top speed close to 12 mph, but the evidence we had just seen suggested that their thickness made little difference.

Nobby had parked the Humber clear of the gulley smell and now noticed the hole in the Bren-gun butt.

'Good job we closed down, else that one might have found your napper.'

I had already offered up my thanks.

A Belgian major commanded one of the HQ Shermans. After a year or more as an attached gunnery expert, he now made his third request in the past two days to be allowed to go forward and look for targets with his Soixante-quinze – the major's usual way of referring to the mounted 75 mm gun. Having twice refused him until the position up front should make more progress, the brigadier conceded this early evening that the major might join one of the leading regiments to see what opportunities presented. Complete with British crew, the stowage bins stuffed with ration sweets saved up to give the major's children when he should liberate Brussels, the solitary tank moved away southward. One tank on its own is no tank, the Oxford tactical course had said. On impulse I sought and received permission to make a rapid visit to my regiment, whose location had earlier come in code over the air, the only communication all day.

We found RHQ harboured in sight of its two squadrons

in an open field with springy turf, an all-round view and no cover. Alastair Hetherington sat at a table, the German-speaking Ernie Ehrenfeld beside him, interrogating one by one a file of prisoners directed from a corner of the field, afterwards redirected to a different corner. In this way all could see that the interrogation was proper and without duress. At the same time no prisoner could hear what questions were being asked until it was his turn. Perhaps it was just name, rank and number, but the paybook would give a unit identification.

Colonel and adjutant seemed relieved to hear from me about the deep gulley and the knocked-out Churchills as evidencing that resistance had been tough. Despite their overt welcome of my visit and news, their underlying restlessness was not hard to sense. The unit had not moved to its intended flank protection positions but it was at immediate readiness. Neighbours had at last captured Rauray during the day but continued resistance in front was keeping all progress slow. If the depth of British penetration so far was four miles, the width was only a mile and a half at most. Now that it was obvious where the corps attack was aiming, the enemy must know just where to concentrate his armoured reserves. The obvious axis for a counter-thrust was north-east, along the ridge to Cheux, slap into the very right flank the regiment would be guarding. How soon could it be expected? Meanwhile B Squadron would not arrive until next month, so Edward Fletcher's recce troop would have to fill any gaps between squadrons with its scoutcars. I thought I caught the general drift of their edginess.

Nobby scrounged a replenishment from the RHQ water cart before we left, and the Humber nosed back into the meadow's end around dusk. The brigadier was upset that the Belgian major and his crew had neither returned nor reached the regiment they had set out for. Nobby and I turned in. No pyjamas for me tonight: anything might happen. I slept but half-woke several times in the night as Allied artillery renewed its assault.

Soon after stand-to and an early breakfast on the 28th,

we moved off with the column, down the far slope of the ridge towards Colleville, soon making a halt in shadow and the morning damp.

When we moved on again, we passed the crewless guns of an enemy field battery, each piece pointing in a different direction. Our path steamed where it emerged into sunlight. A thick line of woods came into view. From the trees on the edge, objects like bundles of rags hung limply, still held fast to boughs by belt straps, the Panzer grenadiers eighteen years old and younger who had sniped at the turrets of Shermans probing this way yesterday.

As the scoutcar rounded a corner of the wood, the Sherman preceding it ground over more bundles, some sprawled half out of slit trenches part collapsed by shell-fire and tank tracks. Nobby and I both thought we saw the occasional grey hand clutching at nothing among the rags. Beyond this point there was another halt. I went forward to the command tank for 'picture'.

The infantry brigade was astride a bridge over the Odon near Tourville. The leading armour was across and pushing on up the far slopes. We should now move down to join them. I was asked whether my regiment had reached its flanking positions. I had to say there was no indication from the radio net whether they had moved at all, but they might be moving under radio silence. I enquired for news of the Belgian major. There was none, but a platoon of infantry had wandered too far left in the night and not returned. They and the Belgian with his crew were all being posted as missing. After all, it was a very narrow bridgehead, although the Jocks were now trying to widen it to the right.

'We're going down to cross the river with the brigade, Nobby. Our own regiment is staying this side and moving out further west. I think I'd better give them a call in case the radio fades down in the valley.'

'Good idea.'

We were already moving onto the main road and distinctly downhill. My call was answered by the CO's operator, his acknowledgement properly minimal.

The valley was heavily treed, undamaged near the road, the Odon itself obscure in the gloom below the small bridge over which so much traffic was passing. Ascending the far slope, the column was soon clear of the trees, quitting the road to move across fields bounded by hedges of varying height, some pointing at a skyline below which numbers of Shermans were deployed and firing. Half-way up, Tac HQ formed open laager, its commander – for the first time on this operation – ordering everyone to dig in.

Nobby and I took turns using the shovel, the one not digging listening to regimental net. This emitted only a very occasional and imperfectly heard message from obscure outstations like ours. Perhaps the squadrons were moving out to flank watch under radio silence. More than once as we exchanged tasks, single bullets cut through the near low hedge. Two ricocheted off the Sherman ten yards in front of us. Tac Brigade was being sniped from the rear. The occasional bullet sounds reminded me of the butts end of a rifle range where targets are checked, pasted up and a score signalled.

Digging became very difficult beyond about three foot down, so we changed over more frequently. When at last we decided our effort would do, Nobby reversed the Humber so that its rear end was just above the trench. We reckoned that by wriggling feet first and on our sides, we could just get in and out without knocking our heads, but we did not rehearse the manoeuvre.

I then took the shovel along the fringe of our field to the left, nearer to where the woods extended further up the hill, seeking a point of comparative seclusion, there to dig a shallow hole, use it, fill in and replace turf afterwards, standard beachhead instructions.

Horseflies settled on my deposit before I could cover it, some apparently choosing to be buried alive. Their presence reminded me that the weather was improved today, really becoming quite hot. Returning to the car, I had the impression – confirmed by Nobby – that sniping had eased up. As soon as I washed my hands, it broke out again, from way off but arriving uncomfortably close.

'It's that towel of yours – too white! You'll get us all shot!!'

Nobby always came straight to the point. I put my towel guiltily away. The sniping shots ceased.

I walked over to the command tank, where the G3 led me to the RAF half-track which, as he said, was about to perform. Brigade armour was trying to reach a summit marked on the map with the figures '112', its height in metres above sea-level, and soon known as 'Hill 112'. Part of one regiment had a toehold on the summit, but from the wood a short way down the far slope, several Tiger tanks were making the hill-top untenable.

The Tigers were thought to be dug in in the wood, probably with alternative firing-positions to which they could move while the trees concealed their manoeuvring. The RAF LO would bring a cab-rank of Typhoons to bear on the wood and blast the Tigers out of their bunkers. The crew of the half-track was already away up the hill to lay a fluorescent arrow on the open ground, while the LO himself was on radio to the airstrips, soon to the cab-rank itself. I gazed at the chimneysweep's broom aerial and the guy wires holding it poised above the HQ.

From near the half-track I could see past the north-west side of Hill 112 and the ridge beyond it that pointed towards Caen city. Through binoculars the whole sector appeared tree-clad, the varied greens of their foliage smothering all identification of dwelling or landmark. To the left of the visual arc, slightly east of north, I estimated the location of Carpiquet, an airfield to which the enemy still denied the Canadians access, far in our rear. No sign of activity there, nor anywhere else below the haze and among the secretive trees.

Reconciling what I was seeing with the map brought alive the wedge our attack was driving across the south-west of William the Conqueror's capital that was also his burial place, a safari over the first of two rivers, while the woods closed in again behind us to hide the dogged elements of Wehrmacht still north, east, south and west of us, with every chance of concentrating effort upon our obvious, held-up spearhead, on Hill 112, just here.

The flight lieutenant was talking into his microphone. There were the Typhoons overhead, twelve of them, circling. A confusion of gun and automatic fire broke out above the noise of their engines: everything the enemy could point upwards was shooting at the planes. None of us had seen rockets fired before. Each hawk in turn pointed itself at the target, dived until the air screamed. We all held our breath. Smoke spurted under each wing, the twin rockets at first keeping pace with the dive, then gaining on it, finally swishing straight for the impact, while the parent craft curved out of the dive so slowly we thought it never could.

The Tiger wood on the far slope of the hill was invisible to us, the sound of detonation taking time to reach our position, but we heard it, twelve times, double ones. The gun and automatic fire continued, but at conclusion of delivery there were twelve Typhoons ranking up to return home.

People patted a modestly smiling flight lieutenant on the back. In the command turret the brigadier was asking his leading colonel on radio if the Shermans could make any progress before the effect wore off. It was soon after this that that colonel's own tank was hit, which he reported as his mount shot from under him, and he transferred to another. No one said how many of his crew had survived with him: it was evidently not a turret hit.

Before the twelfth plane was out of sight, the first of the medium artillery concentration on the invisible wood was fluting over our heads. The G3 stared up at the sky for several seconds.

'There you are! It's true! You can see them at the apex.'

Gazing into the concentrated blue risks a conspiracy of illusion, but soon I too was convinced that we were seeing the occasional 5.5 inch projectile turning slow-motion before plunging down into the Tiger wood.

Going back to the scoutcar, I found Nobby pumping the petrol cooker for lunch. He had received a tin believed to contain Christmas pudding and was proposing to boil it for our main course, if I agreed. It sounded an appetizing change from hardtack on a summer's day.

The headphones hung over the side of the vehicle, a voice so clear it might have been inside the car itself repeating a call-sign in German: *'Sechs Ludwig, sechs Ludwig, sechs Ludwig, kommen, kommen.'* ('Six Ludwig ... come, come.')

Nobby had heard it before, while I was away: 'Cheeky devil, using our net!'

By contrast the regimental broadcasts were faint and difficult to make sense of, but a map reference in code, which might have been the point a squadron had reached or to which it was directed, had me jotting it down with chinagraph pencil on the talc covering my map on its board, then reaching for the day's code card to translate it. Meanwhile we could not hear any reply to Sechs Ludwig's signals, from which I concluded no more than that his transmitter was nearer to us or higher up than whoever it was he was calling.

Assuring Nobby that I should be back before the pudding was ready, I went over to the G3 with the map reference for one part of my regiment. Because they were all north of the river and out to the western flank, I reckoned – and he agreed – that it was not significant to brigade whether the position had been reached yet or not. I reported the full-strength signals of Sechs Ludwig that were dominating my radio net. This was intriguing but neither of us could think how best to exploit it. He would consider the wisdom of reporting the fact to Div. HQ.

I learned from him that the Scotsmen had established a second small bridgehead on our right, at Gavrus. This could explain why sniping from the right rear had stopped. North of the river on the left flank, held since last night by the 43rd (Wessex) Division, enemy infantry and tank attacks had been brought to a halt this morning near Mouen, the area where the Belgian major and the platoon of our infantry had vanished overnight, all very close to the route by which we had crossed the river.

Through the Humber phones, Sechs Ludwig now gave a map reference in clear. I glanced at the grid on my map, confirming that the German one was different.

Nobby took the tin of pudding out of the boiling water, using his towel, which was more brown and black than its original colour. He pierced the metal and removed one end with his can-opener, slid out the fruit-filled pudding until he could cut it in two equal mess-tin portions, passing me mine. We relaxed, one back against each nearside wheel, dug in with our spoons, held the scalding mix in the air for perhaps two seconds to cool it.

It was as that first mouthful was on its way to our eager mouths that a new sound arrested all action. Quite distinct from the continued firing higher up the hill of Sherman guns, it began *fortissimo* and persisted in its crescendo beyond the point of paralysis for all listeners. I have never heard a banshee, but if its effect is to curl the spine, so also did this noise.

After several seconds only our eyes must have moved, because Nobby and I were suddenly looking straight at each other. It broke the spell. As one, we dived for the slit trench, just in time.

The multiple mortar rockets rent the air and the ground above us, always another consignment tearing, rending, shaking the whole earth. The two-ton scoutcar lifted on two wheels, to fall back a foot behind its parked position. When the detonations eventually paused and a fine dust began settling around us, the headphones rang with Sechs Ludwig's unruffled confirmation that all had been bang on target. He asked how many pieces (*Geschütze*) had fired. Still the answers were inaudible.

We crawled out from under the shifted Humber with some difficulty. There was a pronounced dent in the armoured escape door, which was located between the two wheels we had so recently been leaning against. Large chunks of still hot fragmented metal were strewn around. By the ration Sherman, one crew member had a small piece of projectile embedded in his cheek. His mates applied a field dressing until his usual appearance was quite disguised. After moving the car, Nobby found his half of the Christmas pudding in the bottom of the trench, with both our boot imprints in it. Mine took longer to locate, but it had landed some way off, in a cowpat. We were back to hardtack.

Sechs Ludwig spoke again, with a fresh map reference. I squeezed the prestle switch on my microphone to obliterate the second half of it. By the time I released the switch, Sechs Ludwig was no longer speaking. Instead I heard the much fainter voice of my colonel saying that some silly beggar had blocked his transmission and he would now give his instruction to a squadron all over again.

'There you go!' Nobby's face was inscrutable, as always. 'Upsetting the colonel now.'

A second banshee began. We moved resolutely into the slit trench. Then we clambered out again. The noise was less intense this time, the target elsewhere.

This time our own artillery was ready for the rocket assault, and we heard the counter-battery fire going overhead. It was not long before Sechs Ludwig ceased using our frequency, and in periods of comparative quiet I could distinguish occasional regimental reports. Well to the north-west of us, one squadron lost two tanks while engaging an enemy one that was parked in a house, which their gunfire demolished to bury the tank. I made periodic contact when the net was not busy, to reassure the CO that we were intact and on the job, sometimes saying no more than 'Nan Tare Roger' ('Nothing to report').

A Sherman unit from the independent brigade moved up from the bridge behind us and fanned out to the right, disappearing into what cover they could find. We could soon hear some of them opening fire, Browning machine-guns and high-explosive shell. Something had to happen if the attack was to regain momentum. There were at least three miles to go to the second river, the Orne, which the whole operation aimed at crossing to outflank Caen and secure the high ground beyond.

Stuck at Hill 112, Tac HQ could have done with the weight of the whole of that other brigade to effect a penetration to the Orne, but repeated local counter-attacks on the flank north of the river kept the other regiments, as well as our own, engaged back there. So the one unit which had come across to help the armoured brigade could not expect early back-up if it got itself overstretched.

On 28 June in our small bridgehead, we had no details of the build-up of Panzer divisions behind the screen that was already trying to contain us, the factor Charles Pidduck had been musing about two days earlier. 1st SS ('Hitler's Bodyguard') from Belgium had reached Thury Harcourt on the Orne, due south of our position. 9th and 10th SS from Poland (they had halted the Red Army offensive at Tarnopol in April) were assembling south of Aunay-sur-Odon, a mere eleven miles from us. 2nd SS ('Das Reich') from the Toulouse area had gathered further west, at St-Lô, opposite the Americans, but was not yet committed. All four were elite formations superbly equipped with tanks that outgunned ours. Rommel's intention was to use them together for a major counter-strike to the Normandy coast that would split Americans from British and, in Hitler's words, 'drive the British into the sea'. Yet every one of them – as well as the non-SS 2nd and 21st Panzer Divisions – was to contribute significant elements to the task of sealing off our salient and preventing our Orne crossing. Their commitment in this way was to result in Rommel's major strike to the coast never even beginning. Montgomery's determination to retain the initiative was about to achieve its intention, and we were putting it into effect at Hill 112.

Not that I felt much more than an interested spectator just then. I had been useful as a communication link and might be again, but it was understandable that, for the present, both my parent unit and the brigade I was with, separated by nearly four miles, were preoccupied with their respective problems.

Behind the brigade and within the corridor itself, the business of flushing out and dislodging an always aggressive 12th SS went on all day. It had prevented reinforcement of the Scotsmen at Gavrus. But again, at Hill 112 we were unaware of it. Not knowing about the

Panzer build-up and with no repeat of the multiple rocket experience, most personnel at Tac HQ seemed unconcerned at not having moved since morning.

By dusk the cavalry regiment on the summit had been relieved by the Royal Tanks, with the motor battalion dug in to secure it from stalkers in the night. The yeomanry Shermans were close by, protecting the left, while the unit from the other brigade remained deployed to the right towards Esquay and our hill's brother there, labelled '113'.

Our own radio carried little traffic. Nobby and I took our boots off, otherwise sleeping fully dressed. Except for artillery fire, it was a quiet night. But we all stood to, from an hour before dawn.

The morning of the 29th was fine. Good flying-weather for fighter-bombers, the flight lieutenant remarked, as if he knew something.

Nobby and I sensed that the regimental net did not somehow sound its usual serene self. There was nothing tangible to go on. We were not to know that, overnighting back in Cheux, RHQ had suffered from shooting in the dark because of suspected snipers, leading to a calamity in which a barn burned. In our speculation, Nobby was concerned about the recce troop leader, whose voice he had not recently heard on the net. Edward Fletcher had long been a father figure for all the regiment's scoutcar drivers, whether or not they were in recce troop. He cared about them and he had their affection.

An enemy soldier came into Tac HQ lines with his hands up. The paybook and shoulder flashes supported his statement that he was from a six-barrelled mortar unit, probably the one we had received from yesterday. His entire story was that many of his mates had been killed by our counter-battery fire, for which they all had a holy respect. So locally we still had no information about new troop arrivals opposite; if the brigadier and G3 did, they kept their own counsel.

A single Sherman drove from our right front to halt, pointing towards Tac Brigade but well short of the low hedge. From the river bridge came some wheeled seventeen-pounder anti-tank guns, turning left through the Tac HQ cluster to disappear along a narrow track that entered the woods on our left.

Our regimental radio was busier today, not always much clearer than the day before. I strained to listen, made notes of map references or enemy in quantity reported on that crucial right flank four miles distant. A squadron on the approach to Grainville was being shelled and mortared and could see the enemy infantry and a number of Panther tanks, one of which it knocked out, at the cost of two of its own.

On the returned Sherman to our right front, three members of the crew were standing on turret or engine covers, in conversation with someone hidden from view in the turret itself. From somewhere in our field another soldier appeared to help them. Straps were produced and lowered into the cupola, fastened, then pulled upon gently until a large human form partly covered in a blanket emerged from the hatches. Two crew relinquished the upper straps to take a better hold on the body, boots staggered and slipped on the metal rim of the drop. At last the dead tank commander was laid, with every attempt at reverence, across the engine covers. Two crew began sewing him into a pair of blankets. The others descended to begin digging a first resting-place. In half an hour an officer and a padre had arrived by jeep, and a service was conducted for the interment.

The day was now really hot. On the hill, the armoured regiments had persisted with their tasks all morning against continuing resistance, but it took until after noon before the motor battalion and one Sherman unit gained possession of the Tiger wood on the far slope of the hill. This made it possible to deploy a second regiment, for the first time to the east of the hill, where a road ran north-east between the two rivers in the direction of Caen.

The G3 had just confided that, if the armour continued to be held up, the general planned for the infantry brigade to hold on to what had been gained … He was interrupted by a message, after which he remarked that the unit on the right – the one on loan from the other brigade – was now progressing again. It had just reached the Esquay–Evrecy road at a point where it overlooked both places.

As if their advance were a signal, suddenly we heard all hell being let loose at them. My watch said just after 2.30 when a fusillade of high-velocity gunfire began pushing armour-piercing projectiles over our position. The target was clearly the unit on the right – which lost six tanks in the very first salvo – but the 'overs' were disconcerting enough, and there was no let-up.

Everyone at Tac Brigade moved quickly into the vehicles. Engines started. Through the feathering shot and occasional earth burst of high explosive, we all moved off in our usual order up to the lateral track, following it to the left into the cover from view of the wooded area. Brigadier Roscoe Harvey stood up in the turret of his Sherman, parked in the open where we turned onto the track and facing the enemy with its dummy gun. As each of us passed him, conspicuous in his red-banded hat, he shouted pleasantly at us to keep our heads down.

Once inside the fringe of the wood, some vehicles continued along the track, others swung off it where there were spaces between trees. I spotted a large mound of earth to the right, and Nobby happily steered the Humber off into its lee. The mound proved to be surmounted by a memorial cross and to contain a representation of the Virgin and babe to watch over our vehicle.

'That's nice!' Nobby nodded at the figure as he struggled out of the driver's hatch. Once his feet were on the ground, he wrested the Bren gun from its clamp, checked the magazine, went to a bin where he kept others. As he seemed happy preparing our personal defence, I said I should take a look round and come back to join him.

There was no doubt in my mind that the enemy had just begun a major counter-attack. It was perhaps inevitable that I should remember Alastair's story of the Tiger tanks that had appeared out of the woods at Villers-Bocage to shoot up that leading Desert Rat unit earlier in the month.

What now exercised me was how long would the Panzers take to blast their way through to where we were, or whether the unit they were attacking would succeed in holding them.

I walked to the fringe of the trees in time to see the brigadier's tank, escorted by one other, drive off up the hill towards one of the regiments. The overs were still feathering and whining by but the trees afforded some sense of comparative security. There was now the additional noise of the German fast-firing machine-guns, delivering their startling short bursts, but no sign that the bullets were reaching this far yet.

In a hedgerow facing the direction of fire, I came upon one of the seventeen-pounders dug in for business. Nobby would be glad to hear we had one of those between us and the enemy attack. The gun crew seemed to have a bombardier in charge. I asked him if his officer was anywhere about. He had not seen him for perhaps an hour. Where was the next gun? He thought it was quite a long way along the hedge, down the hill. What did I think was happening? I said it seemed like quite a serious counter-attack using tanks. It would probably have to work its way through the whole of the armoured regiment on that flank before he would get anything in his sights. I was sure he knew the difference between a Panther and a Sherman, but if he had any doubts or worries, mine was the first scoutcar down the track and I'd be on call to him.

As I walked back to the car, I passed people from Tac Brigade vehicles who had their pistols or rifles at the ready and were peering down the track as if the enemy might appear at any moment. They could be right.

Nobby had set up the Bren on the engine cover, cocked, pointing back along the track. Having decided that nothing worse was going to happen for at least ten minutes, he was pouring each of us a mug of steaming thermos tea. I took a first hot sip before ducking across the track to explore a farmyard entrance opposite. There was the flight lieutenant, whose face lit up at my appearance. He was grappling with the components of his giant aerial in a tangle of support wires.

'That move really caught us on the hop. Look at the mess!'

His crew were sorting out the jumbled contents of the half-track now parked in a dark half-barn. I gave him a hand with the tangle around the sweep's broomsticks. He was desperately keen to erect them and re-establish contact with his base. I asked if the thing would work well enough without putting the mast up so high that it showed above the tree-tops.

'Why?' Then the penny dropped. 'Christ! You don't think they're close enough to see it?'

'I wouldn't gamble on it.'

From further back the enemy would probably beam on his signal with locators as soon as he broadcast anyway; no point in letting the Panzer troops see the mast as well. We compromised by erecting the thing to just below tree-top level. He called his crew to get things connected up. I said my tea would be getting cold and went back to the Humber. The tank battle was still raging, the noise thickened up now by high-explosive shells bursting, although some of these sounded further west and nearer to the river, behind us almost.

'What's happened to the brigadier?' The flight lieutenant had followed me across the track to ask. I pointed up the hill.

Communication with our local commander was not going to be simple: the LO would try to raise him on one of his smaller sets. Before he went, he asked me, lowering his voice, if the enemy should penetrate this far, what had we best do, drive further along the track? I reckoned that way would soon run slap into some more foe: it was a very small bridgehead. As an old infantier – and only *if* the enemy was upon us, I should favour detuning my radio, immobilizing the Humber and walking down through the woods to the river to look for a way to cross after dark. I should, of course, take Nobby and the Bren. The RAF crew would be welcome to join us if they would only try to move quietly. The LO said right, that's what we would do if it came to it, and went back to call up the brigadier.

Nobby had been trying to hear above the din what was happening to our distant regiment; he thought A Squadron had reported being shot at by some Shermans, from some formation they had not seen before.

Because the battle was intensifying, seemingly broadening its front behind us, some people along the track were looking fidgety. Then, from the direction of the bridge, one Cromwell tank on its own drove along the fringe of the wood at perhaps 25 mph, braking to a halt athwart the track, the miniature yellow pennant with its virile black bull displayed at turret top. Two heads showed above the hatches, the divisional general and Charles.

'Hallo, Keith!' Charles called as if he had been expecting me to be just there. 'Where's the brigadier?'

'You can just see him near the top.' I pointed.

'Pip' Roberts, youngest armoured division commander in the British Army, spoke into his microphone. The engine roared. They were away. An old saying of my favourite aunt recurred to me: 'One above sees all.'

It took perhaps ten minutes before the sheer volume of British artillery, field, medium and heavy, crashed out from a wide arc well behind us, and kept on and on and on. From Hill 112 fire was being directed on the seen and the unseen enemy in and out of the many woods from which the 10th SS Panzer Division was hitting not only the single armoured regiment on our right but the Scots bridgehead at Gavrus.

The Scotsmen had had no tanks to support them, nor anti-tank guns except their own few six-pounders, which they had manhandled along the abominably sticky river bank from the first bridge – the one we had crossed – at Tourville. Most of both divisions' anti-tank artillery was deployed further north to guard the right-flank ridge, correctly judged to be the route for the biggest counter-thrust, which began at about 6 p.m.

At brigade the 'six o'clock' was scarcely noticed. This was partly because, nearer to us, the cacophony of onslaught stemming from Bougy area on our right kept being renewed. The infantry and tank attacks on Gavrus were so persistent that by 9 p.m. one company was withdrawn to join others nearer the two bridges where the river splits. Yet how the evening counter-thrust progressed was crucial: its aim was to cut off the bridgehead completely.

The weight of artillery fire that the general had called down sent any Panzers back into cover, which at once eased our local and right-front threat. It also disrupted the forming-up areas from which attacks were sustained, areas identifiable only once the direction of attack showed itself. Aircraft made telling use of opportunities along approach roads to the areas, because this counter-attack was so important to the enemy – ordered by Hitler himself from Berchtesgaden – that many columns and supplies moved in daylight.

Despite all gunnery and air-strike effort, the six o'clock operation rolled forward on schedule. It had two axes, one along the road from Villers-Bocage towards Caen, the other up the ridge from Noyers towards Cheux. Using 9th SS, with Panzer Lehr on their left, and a battle group from 2nd SS with help from 2nd Panzer on the right axis, the enemy drive attacked the flank for which the two squadrons of our regiment shared responsibility. Nobby and I were alerted to the scene by the stepped-up activity – not too clearly heard most of the time – on regimental net.

At about dusk, when Tac HQ had already quit the lateral track (and Nobby and I our shrine) and laagered close to its original position but more on the fringe of the woods, the regiment's two squadrons seemed to be receiving orders to move forward. We had inferred that until then they had been static and firing at counter-attack forces from cover. As the light faded, so radio reception became at times clearer. Then at other times it would fade, so our picture was the more confused. Only later did we learn that the regiment had come under command of the 4th Armoured Brigade, whose new brigadier – Michael Carver, most certainly of that legendary regimental stock, a 'black beret' – had logically ordered both squadrons forward to give direct support and security to the Scots infantry positioned in front of them and closer to the axes of counter-attack.

The colonel sounded impatient that neither squadron had yet begun its move, when it was now almost dark. A rear-link captain accused the CO of clowning, keeping one squadron waiting while he tried to contact the other. It was A Squadron that had gone off the air. The CO persisted in asking the link to report his signals.

Eventually, much like three days before, Major Robert Peel himself responded. Very deliberately he said that, if the colonel were up there with them, he would understand. On the start-line they were receiving non-stop airbursts and heavy mortar fire. The net faded and revived – was it something about a tank and crew that had vanished into the dark? The rest of the squadron had received the order and was ready, but it was pitch black and there were Jerries all round.

'Very well then,' – from the CO – 'get on with it!'

The other squadron must already have moved. It now cut in to report a close-quarters tank engagement, Cromwells versus Mark IV's crossing the path of their advance, in the darkness illuminated only by the exchange of gunfire. The CO acknowledged, then at once asked A Squadron to confirm it had moved. There was no reply. The colonel tried again, several times. It seemed probable that no set in the squadron was now tuned to RHQ and that the harassed commander was full-time in touch with his troops on the other frequency. At last the major had evidently flicked to regiment, because he suddenly announced that they were moving as ordered and that everything was shooting at their exhaust flames.

'Goodbye, Colonel!'

The finality of the words was emphasized when neither squadron used the net in the next considerable while. No doubt every set would be on intercom to control the immediate situation.

I left a mesmerized Nobby on radio watch while I went

to report to the brigadier that my regiment was effecting a night advance on the right flank, that I had received no map references of their objectives, that the net was at present quiescent.

The brigadier was not visible. The G3 took my information, remarking that things were a bit fluid all round. He was expecting the senior LO back from a risky night trip to division with fresh written orders for us on the hill.

As I returned to the Humber, I knew that Nobby would be sweating about what on earth had happened to our regiment. At the same time, neither of us could be too certain what was likely to happen, south of the Odon, to us.

Allied artillery was working late, pounding the identified enemy concentrations. We heard this as a background noise but locally experienced periods of comparative quiet. My eyes had adjusted to the gloom, which I found very far from pitch dark. In fact, it seemed one or two stars were appearing.

As Nobby had nothing fresh on radio, I took the shovel to the fringe of the wood to accomplish something there had been no opportunity for all day. Noticing an abandoned vee trench clear of the trees and already partly filled in, I decided to save effort in digging. I had just completed essentials and was purposefully unwinding a toilet roll when something swished through the night air, almost unhurriedly, and exploded close to the other end of the trench. I jumped down into cover at some point midway between where the 56 mm mortar bomb had burst and where I had just been stooping, actually laughing in unbelief and feeling ludicrous.

Five minutes later nothing further had happened, and with dress adjusted I returned to Tac Brigade. I remembered reading a report last winter of small mortar sniping enthusiasts among our opponents. And at night! He must have been part of a patrol that was seeing at least as well in the dark as I could, perhaps better.

The senior LO, Basil Gibson, returned. The whole

brigade, including the regiment on loan, was to quit the bridgehead during the night, leaving it for the infantry brigade with divisional anti-tank gun support to hold the line of woods, but not Hill 112.

All night long the little river bridge was busy with Shermans trying to move quietly. Tac Brigade pulled out in the small hours and I was released to link up once more with my regiment.

Up the far hill I made radio contact with RHQ, received in code a rendezvous (RV) point that was well to the north. As the sky lightened, we were driving back along the way that had been so much under threat. In the opposite direction long files of fresh Welsh infantry, the 53rd, were moving up to make sure the gains of the Scotsmen and ourselves stayed firm. I thought how clean they looked. Some nodded at me non-committally, as people who go to work early in the morning greet each other in the fraternity conferred by the hour. But I, who had trained for infantry, was moving back. I did not know then that in this recent push the casualties in the Scottish Division, which had shouldered the biggest part, were 2,500.

At the RV point, still before full daylight, I joined the regimental second-in-command, Major Lord George Montague-Douglas-Scott, who said I might help him harbour the regiment when it came in, if I would. The two scoutcars, abreast, faced across the track where the tanks would come into the area allocated. I switched off radio. The 2 I/C's radio continued to hum after he spoke on it briefly to the CO. The drivers sat silent in the depths of the vehicles. Silent too the major and I, perched on the respective rear hatches, contriving to keep straight backs, neither of us having slept a wink for twenty-four hours.

After an age, the positive engine note of Cromwells. C Squadron began to come in, almost together, incomplete, all commanders tight-lipped, determined to see their vehicles to the allotted places, acknowledging no one. Then a substantial number of Daimler scoutcars from the recce troop. Watching the last one come by, I broke silence to the major.

'Where's Edward?'

I think he blinked, his ordinarily hollow-eyed expression becoming gloomier than usual.

'Stepped on a mine. He won't walk again; that's if he lives.'

If I was shaken by this reply, I could only guess at Nobby's reaction in the dimness of the driving-seat.

When RHQ came by, there was no sign of the adjutant. Finally, up to seven tanks of A Squadron straggled in, long gaps between arrivals, the crews haggard, dirty, exhausted. The small open harbour had space to spare.

This was our regiment, the 2nd Northamptonshire Yeomanry, at that time on the morning of 30 June after a four-day action, the unit I had been with for no more than a year, to which I had only recently begun to feel I was making an accepted contribution, to belong there.

We had to hope more crews would arrive later on. As the next-to-last tank of A Squadron drove past the two scoutcars, I saw it through a shifting aqueous mist, became aware that my shoulders were heaving in great unashamed, uncontrollable sobs.

4 Cows and Cannon Fire

Next day in a new harbour area near the Caen–Bayeux road, my greatest need was for a bath. The water cart had joined us. Digging a shallow hole in the robust turf and spreading my groundsheet in it, I poured in the water from two jerricans, refilled both from the cart, stripped off and stepped into the home-made pond glistening in the morning sunlight, all nine gallons of it. The echelon had brought my new tablet of soap and first change of clothing.

I was still towelling dry when Nobby appeared from another part of RHQ.

'Colonel's asking to see Lieutenant Jones, sir.'

His tone was unusually solemn, but next minute he asked if he could use my bathwater to give his towel its initial wash. I dressed quickly and set out for the CO's mobile command post, a kind of outsize motor-caravan that normally stayed back with the echelon.

Seven Cromwells of A Squadron had failed to return, including the squadron commander's. Whilst C Squadron had reached their infantry along the railway line near Grainville and remained until dawn as ordered, A Squadron had overshot theirs in the dark and landed in an enemy position, where their reception was predictably explosive. On radio the OC had twice asked permission to withdraw, had been twice refused. Around 1 a.m. on the 30th signals had ceased. Thirty-five members of the regiment were now posted as 'missing'.

The adjutant, Bobby Lorimer, was not missing. A kindly arrangement, it was said, had taken him as soon as the unit was released from flank duty to a telephone connected cross-Channel for a personal conversation following the arrival of his first-born. Bobby's was the regiment's one piece of good news, for we now heard that Edward had not survived.

As I approached the caravan, feeling so much better for the cold bath, I was quite expecting the 'Old Man' to tell me which units I was to contact for the next action. When I entered, he was quite alone – Lieutenant-Colonel D.A.R.B. Cooke. He came straight to the point.

'Good morning, Keith. I want you to move to A Squadron and take over the rear link.'

Of course, he had to restructure his unit ready for its next engagement. My infantry seniority was to count. I should have foreseen it. I waited to hear more.

'You've done a good job as LO. You don't waffle on the air. That's what I want on regimental net, a quick, full picture of what's going on. Your promotion to captain will come through and be back-dated to today. You know John MacGillicuddy – he'll be your squadron commander.'

He must have read my face. 'Big Mac', as I thought of him, had until now been second-in-command of C Squadron. When I had been posted there on arrival a year ago, he and I had failed to 'hit it off'. Becoming RLO some months later, which I saw as a positive change, had the added advantage that his path and mine no longer crossed daily. But now …

'I know what some of you feel about John, but he is the senior captain, an experienced officer and generous, done a lot for the men. This is your chance to start working with him. The squadron second-in-command will be Tony Venner. You get on all right with him, don't you?'

'Yes, sir.'

'Move over after lunch then. Good luck!'

When I reached A Squadron, its new commander took me at once to the rear-link tank. He introduced the lance-corporal radio-operator, Bill, as one of the best in the regiment, then left me to meet the rest of the crew and get sorted out.

Bill introduced the others. He was the only one without a distinctive dialect: driver Albert was Cockney, Harry the co-driver from a Norfolk farm, Stanley the gunner a Yorkshireman. I said they probably knew I had been the regimental liaison officer so had not yet commanded a tank in action, nor much at all. I hoped we'd get on.

The tank, Bill cautioned me, smelled strongly inside at present. They had arrived back only this morning from where the fitters had pumped out as best they could, then tried to swill out with formalin, which had its own pervasive odour.

'They say it wears off.'

Stanley thought the smell today was a mix of the disinfectant with what was left of the blood. It was preferable to just the smell of the blood on its own – they'd had a night of that, when he was pinned to his perch on the gunner's stool and the only view of outside was through the telescope, which did not work in the dark.

'He was a big chap, our officer,' in a West Riding accent.

'Had plenty of blood in him,' in East Anglian.

'The old girl stank rotten,' from London.

They were trying to tell me something that I might have expected to hear first from Big Mac, who surely must have known – or did he?

'When the airburst hit him, he was standing on the commander's pedestal,' Stanley explained.

'Head and shoulders outside the cupola.' Bill had seen him out of his own open hatches. Lucky the airburst had not caught him too, but he was below roof-level at that moment, attending to the radio.

'I felt his knees sag into my back and I was stuck there. And his shoulders must have jammed in the hatches with his arms still outside. From then on, he just bled all down me onto the turret floor, for hours and hours.'

'I drove her out.' Albert's leadership potential showed as he took up the story. All four were living the time over again; it was not forty-eight hours old.

'We had to get the commander out,' Bill explained, 'just couldn't do it where we were; everything was shooting at us. He was unconscious, but whether wounded or already dead he was also kneeling on Stanley. We were no use to the squadron in that state. I agreed with Albert, let's get back and sort ourselves out.'

For me, the penny was dropping: Major Peel's message that faded, about a tank and crew that vanished into the dark.

'Albert did a brilliant job, getting us back,' Bill asserted.

'Bill cleaned some of the blood off the map board, but it was dark, daren't show a light.'

'At first I was scared we'd be bazooka'd by the enemy. Then later I was worried our own troops, if we ever reached them, might think we were a Tiger.'

Scared or not, Bill and Albert had worked as a team. In enforced passivity, Harry and Stanley had shared every testing moment with them. Swerving or stopping at every shadow that moved or looked suspicious, a journey perhaps under five miles had taken an endless time.

'As it happened, we were dead lucky with our own troops, but I thought we'd never get there, or I'd cave in first. As soon as we stopped, I thought they'd take the load off my back, but first go they couldn't shift him. Our officer had gone all stiff.'

For the first time I looked deliberately up at the turret. What I saw confirmed the explanation forming in my mind. This was A Squadron's original rear-link tank and crew! The turret cupola still carried the customized paraphernalia by which major and captain had communicated every time their tanks were halted for more than a few minutes. On each occasion they would run out a length of cable from a drum on the rear link and plug it into the socket of a cable in the major's tank. With this umbilical cord connected, the major had two-way access to regimental net without having to flick frequencies on his own set, which sometimes meant retuning. The same gimmick achieved that he or his operator was never out of touch with the five troops on the squadron frequency.

The device that had worked so brilliantly in several models of tank on exercises in Britain inevitably met snags in the harsher environment of real warfare. Whenever a sudden move was necessary (for instance, if a heavy mortar concentration straddled Squadron HQ), the cable still had to be unplugged and reeled in or lost for ever. The drum itself obstructed vision out of the rear-link cupola. It also restricted rapid entry and egress. The captain had not been large. Perhaps he had practised not knocking his brains or other parts on the monstrosity as he got in and out. Not so his successor!

I saw it all now. The captain had left this tank and crew on the 26th, when the second-in-command was sniped, and had transferred to Wyvil Raynsford's vehicle. In the short break between the initial engagement on the 26th and the move out to flank on the 28th (twenty-four hours later than expected), a troop leader, whom Harry and Stanley could only name as 'our officer', had been taken away from his troop and his usual tank and put into this one with the cable and drum, where at dusk on the 29th an airburst killed him.

I looked hard at my crew. What an experience they had shared! I pointed at the cable drum and its connections.

'Would it upset you much if we got rid of that contraption?'

Bill's response was generous; Albert waxed enthusiastic about dismantling it. I formally asked John Mac's permission. He nodded consent. I was agreeably surprised at this reply, however casually he gave it. I signed thumbs-up to Albert, who went to work at once.

My crew was an established team, on first-name terms all the time. Albert's surname was Larkin, I think Harry's was Dawson. Was Bill a Davies? And what, I try in vain to recall, was Stan's other name? Themselves were unforgettable.

That night a sentry patrolling squadron lines had a mishap with his Sten gun, shot himself in the leg.

As the stench in the tank diminished – or as we all became more accustomed to it, I spent more time in the turret. Being inside a tank has something in common with the kind of prison cell in which you are lowered down through a hole in the roof, which is also the only way out. A tank is not so deep as a cell. When you stand in army boots on the revolvable floor, your forehead is just below the cupola ring, if your height is almost six foot. To step up onto the Cromwell pedestal raised you about a foot, enough to collect an airburst or a sniper's bullet. There was a small leather-covered stool projecting from the turret ring, onto which you could hook yourself for a change of posture and a further elevation. Finally, when not at immediate risk as a target, a commander could park his bottom on the rim of the cupola, with the hatch lids open one each side protecting his thighs from small-arms fire or a sudden squall. If you preferred to have your hatches open fore and aft, like those on the operator's side, there was a simple bolt to pull back on the cupola, which would then traverse to the desired position and bolt into a hole drilled at ninety degrees from the previous one.

Driver and co-driver each had their separate hatches in the two forward corners of the hull. It was possible to pass something forward or back from their compartment to the turret, and in a real emergency to crawl through. The turret gunner was in front of the commander, so nearest to the co-driver when the turret was traversed front. The gunner normally got in and out by the commander's cupola. For all concerned, entrance and exit were something they were used to, so long as they stayed alive and athletic. For a wounded crew member, getting out was another matter. If in the rear link we thought about it, we also avoided discussing it. Yet we could expect to find, like all other crews, that when a tank is hit, the motivation to bale out is a reflex action, like the corks in five bottles simultaneously drawn – provided, that is, all five are unimpaired.

Tony Venner, who arrived to be squadron second-in-command, had spent the first action back in the reinforcement holding unit. He brought a new 95 mm close-support gun Cromwell and crew to replace the one in Wehrmacht hands. Tony had been in C Squadron when I joined it on the Yorkshire Wolds the previous summer, so I reckoned he had had rather longer to get to know Big Mac. One leave he had got married, to a French bride, whom he brought once only to the squadron mess. Now he gave me a few tips about managing a tank turret. Tony's specialism was gunnery, whereas the courses on which C Squadron had sent me were for driving and maintenance, one on the Cromwell, the other on the American Stuart, or Honey, a light tank which the regiment did not have.

An event at the beginning of July that was in part distinctly related to our recent first action was the compulsory retirement of Field Marshal von Rundstedt, the enemy commander in the West. On the first day of our attack Hitler had summoned him and Rommel, who commanded the army group opposing us, to Berchtesgaden to listen and not to be listened to. By the time the pair got back to France, our visible dent in the line had been made and also sealed off at the price of committing all the Panzer reserves. From his near-Paris HQ, von Rundstedt telephoned Keitel to urge the Führer to make peace with the West so as to concentrate all forces for defence of the East.

Next day Hitler sent him quite a nice letter – for him, effectively saying, 'Poor old man, retire and have a well-earned rest.' The 'old man' had, after all, been in charge of all the most spectacular incursions of armoured forces from the Reich, into Poland, across France and to that furthest point of all, Rostov-on-Don. Rundstedt would have commanded the invasion of Britain if it had not been called off. Even now Hitler was to use the retirement to have the FM conduct 'courts of honour' to turn over other resisting generals to the usually fatal processes of the 'people's courts'.

Von Rundstedt's replacement was von Kluge, not fully recovered from a vehicle accident on the Eastern Front, the commander whose troops had clawed their way into the suburbs of Moscow in time for the 1941 freeze-up. He was known to his soldiers as 'Clever Hans' and came to

Normandy confident of putting things right. Not one word of this change reached us in the regiment at that time, and if the bare fact filtered through to us later, its insidious significance was lost on us. In fact, from the persistently savage nature of enemy resistance, we might have been forgiven had we inferred there was *no* significance.

We thought we were winning the war, even if our invasion just now was a bit static. Those of us who had folks in London knew about the nightly salvoes of V1 rockets and looked forward to a move eastward to put the bases out of action.

The various promotions came through in due course, including a second stripe for Bill. On 8 July the regiment moved to some high ground in the general area of Cristot and Le Mesnil Patry, with the task of counter-attacking any further enemy push up the ridge past Rauray towards the beaches. There on the 12th B Squadron joined us from Britain.

RHQ was established in a cornfield, A upon fairly short grass. As the squadron drove into position on the first day, a herd of black-and-white cows ambled off over the lip of the plateau that had apparently been serving them as pasture, down the rough bracken and bush-strewn slope that led into a broad valley before rising again to the tree-concealed ridge on the far side. The cattle strayed only perhaps a third of the way down. Once the Cromwells' Rolls-Royce engines were silent, the beasts began a sauntering return trip, soon infiltrating the steel invaders.

Harry recognized their predicament at once: 'Die if they're not milked!'

Allocation was made of one cow per tank, with Harry giving instruction in milking to the majority who were ignorant of the art. The herd settled down amicably with us, while crews dug pits in the hard ground and drove the tanks astride them to afford shelter for sleeping. Was it because the nearest enemy was perhaps four miles off and we had to stay mobile for instant counter-attack that we left the camouflage nets folded in their bins?

No signs of former occupation by the enemy were to be seen on the hill-top, but about as far down the slope into the valley as the cows had gone that first day was a small trench system still identified by the Wehrmacht's customary marker sticks. Thinking they had been dug on the south-east side as part of all-round defence and probably not used, I walked down to look. They were indeed deserted, weaponless, clean. As I was about to leave, I noticed a grubby piece of paper held down on the parapet by a large pebble. On it in pencil was a list of names – of an infantry section? – and against most of them the letters 'gef.', presumably an abbreviation for '*gefallen*'.

Gefallen … dead … I wrote daily to my adored spouse – when I could, and she to me as often, although in both directions letters tended to arrive in batches. I think all the squadron wrote letters home, the rule being that most events could be related provided that fourteen days had elapsed since they happened. In censoring others' letters I had set about schooling myself to scan them for breaches of security without taking in the very personal and private messages. At an average age just below our mid-twenties, we were all adult, and breaches were few.

When the farmer eventually discovered his cows and drove them off from our midst, he seemed not in the least pleased to find them alive, nor grateful to those who had kept them so by regular milking. Some crews had actually tethered their prize, not that they were other than helpful and friendly in releasing them when the farmer appeared. Like the labourer on the bicycle in the long wood, the farmer not only did not attempt to speak to us but affected to remove his happy beasts as if he had not seen us there.

Admittedly we had encountered very few civilians so far, but those we had gave us the uneasy feeling that they had not asked for liberation and wished we had never left home. No doubt we were driving tanks across their ripening crops, the artillery putting shell-holes everywhere, leaving some cattle dead. Our coming meant that the enemy's peaceful coastal troops had departed, sometimes with the farmers' horses, carts and poultry. In the minds of the Norman farming population there must still have been the question whether the forces of the Third Reich would return, overwhelming the present invaders.

The only form in which we saw the enemy during our counter-attack role was the Luftwaffe. We had become so accustomed to our side's air superiority that a series of assaults on our uncamouflaged plateau by Messerschmidt 109s firing their 20 mm cannon into us came as a surprise, but everyone dived smartly enough for cover.

After the first wave had gone, I asked Stanley to set up the Bren gun on its bipod, loaded, on the tank engine covers. When the second attack was approaching across the valley, I grabbed the gun, pulled back the action, then squeezed the trigger, intending to show off my infantry-trained prowess and hosepipe a line of tracer into the leading machine. All that happened was that the working parts slid quietly forward, and not even one shot was emitted. With practised speed I pulled back the cocking handle, removed magazine, pressed trigger, pulled back, mag on, fired again. The result was the same as before. The last plane had now gone.

I took off the magazine, picked out a first cartridge with a struggle, then used its point to force the rest out one by one. Eventually thirty rounds lay on the ground in front of me.

'Who filled this magazine?'

'I did,' said Stanley, 'I expect.'

'How many rounds do you put in a Bren mag?'

'As many as it'll take. I reckon I got near thirty into most of them.'

'Did you fire a Bren gun course?'

'No, I've only ever learned tank Besas, fill the belt.'

'Did no one ever say you don't put more than twenty-one in a Bren magazine, especially if it's going to be some time before you fire them?'

'Not that I can recall. Why is that then?'

'The spring isn't up to more. That's why this lot just jammed. If our lives had depended on that gun firing, we'd now all be dead.'

'Oh dear! I'm sorry. Had I better unload all the others and refill 'em with twenty-one apiece?'

'Yes please, Stanley.'

He climbed to the turret to get some more magazines.

'I'll bet you're fed up with me?'

'Dear old Sergeant Sheppard of the Hampshire depot would have said I was the one firing the gun, so it was up to me to check it. Just now he'd be disappointed in me.'

I was several tanks away when the next strike came in, and I dived for cover with the rest. One or two Bofors guns were heard firing nearby this time, and one Messerschmidt crashed in an adjoining field.

Some of us took a walk that far before dusk. The pilot was still strapped in, dead, his face an unnatural bronzy brown. Surprising his crew-mates, Albert launched an impulsive kick at the damaged fuselage next to the corpse, muttering that it was retaliation for flattening the family home back in London. Harry reproached him: a dead man could do no more harm, would never again in this world milk a cow.

During this interlude between major engagements for the regiment, 120 Soviet divisions with 5,000 tanks and 6,000 ground-support aircraft continued blasting an enormous hole in German Army Group Centre, inflicting a loss of twenty-eight out of its forty divisions, with 300,000 casualties. I cannot now recall our hearing this ongoing news saga at the time – statistics like these could hardly fail to make an impression if they had been given – nor any discussion of it. Did we hear about it? Were we so preoccupied with our own part of the war, the slow progress from the beach-head, the news from home about the V1 attacks, the awareness of our first casualties in killed, wounded and missing, after a clear four years in the sceptred isle away from the shooting war? Were our minds at work on the now known vulnerability of our tanks to enemy 75 and 88 mm guns and bazookas? Yet our morale was already higher than before that first action. Perhaps we did hear of a Soviet breakthrough and reacted that we had better do better?

5 Bull, Eye and Rat

On 16 July we were briefed for next action. Mac came back from RHQ and told his officers. The troop leaders told their troops. I told the rear link crew.

We were to set out from the small bridgehead east of the River Orne and its canal connecting Caen to the sea. Three British armoured divisions would sweep south to dominate (Montgomery's word) the high ground in the area around Bourgebus, the same objective as our division had had – but not reached – in its June action. A thousand British bombers would precede the attack by neutralizing both flanks with high explosive. Almost as many American planes would then overfly our intended assault corridor to treat the fortified villages with fragmentation bombs. After that 400 guns – including the Royal Navy's – would support us forward as far as they could reach.

'Sounds pretty marvellous,' was Bill's comment when I had finished.

'Three armoured divisions; how many tanks?' Albert queried.

'Around 700 cruisers, a mix of Shermans and Cromwells.'

'A thousand bombers! What'll they be, Lancasters?' Stanley mused. 'That's a lot of high explosive, makes big craters. I hope they drop it in the right places, and not on us.'

'Don't forget the Yanks,' Harry reproved him. 'They're much more likely to drop their fragmentation bombs in the wrong place.'

'All the same,' – Bill was not smiling – 'it's tremendous

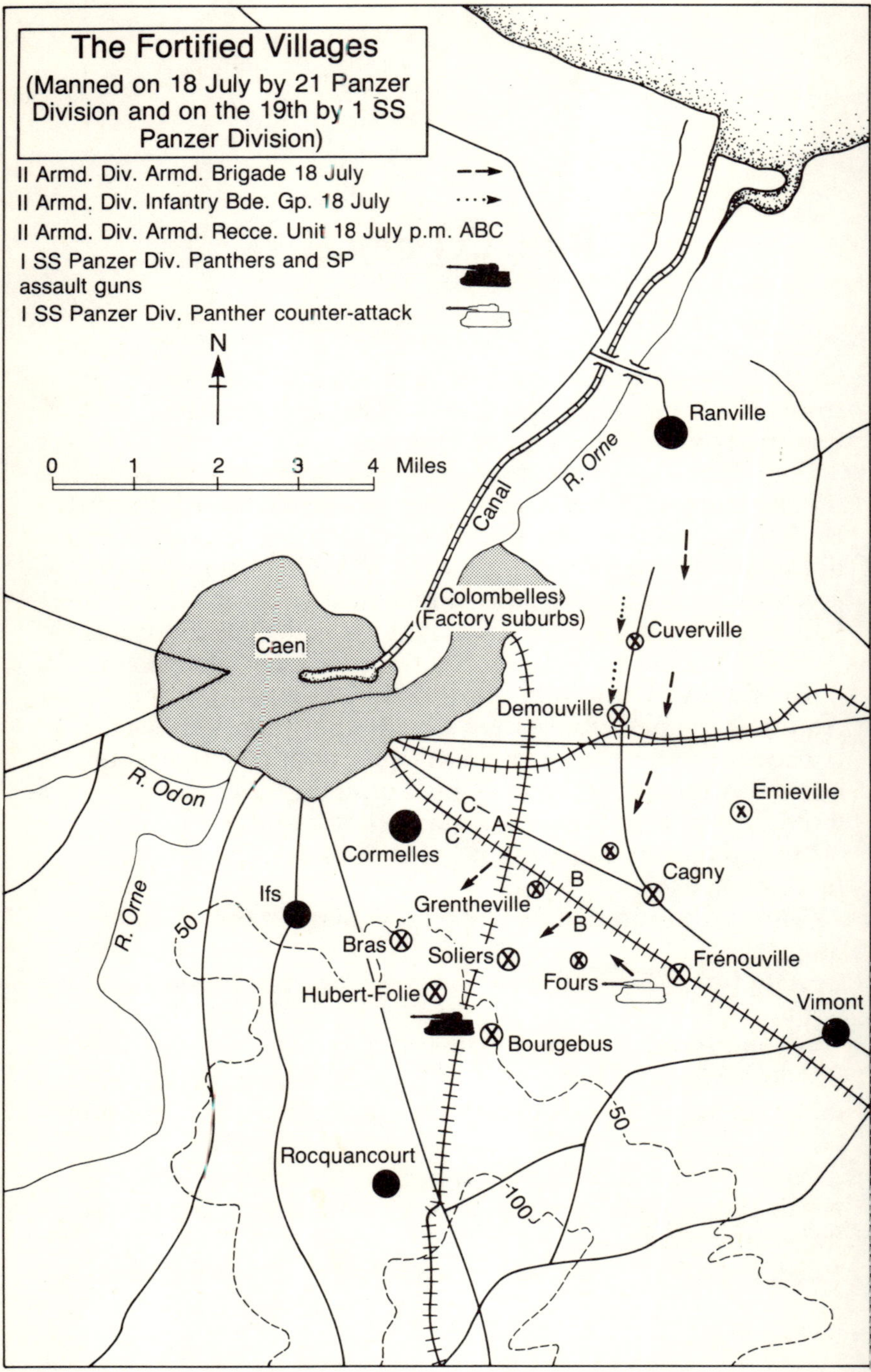
The Fortified Villages
(Manned on 18 July by 21 Panzer Division and on the 19th by 1 SS Panzer Division)
II Armd. Div. Armd. Brigade 18 July
II Armd. Div. Infantry Bde. Gp. 18 July
II Armd. Div. Armd. Recce. Unit 18 July p.m. ABC
I SS Panzer Div. Panthers and SP assault guns
I SS Panzer Div. Panther counter-attack
N
0
1
2
3
4
Miles
Ranville
R. Orne
Canal
Colombelles
(Factory suburbs)
Caen
Cuverville
Demouville
Emieville
R. Odon
C
A
C
Cormelles
Cagny
B
Grentheville
B
Ifs
R. Orne
50
Bras
Soliers
Frénouville
Fours
Hubert-Folie
Vimont
Bourgebus
50
Rocquancourt
100

support, if it all works out.'

Harry had been thinking: 'Sounds almost too good to be true. Makes you wonder where the snag is.'

There was so much that we did not know. Not that it would have made any difference.

'Are all the 700 tanks setting off at once?' Albert wanted to know.

I told him from the map that the bridgehead was barely ten square miles – say, four long by two-and-a-bit wide – still packed, as far as I knew, with 6th Airborne, who had secured it on D-Day, and 51st Highland, who had tried to extend it at the time 7th Armoured was running into trouble at Villers-Bocage, just before we had disembarked. It was also to accommodate the 3rd Division, Monty's own at the time of Dunkirk, to secure left flank and capture Troarn. I reckoned there would be room for only one armoured division at a time.

'So who goes first?'

It was a good question.

'We do.'

Among the things we did not know was that, after our previous push had been sealed off at Hill 112, Montgomery had urged General Bradley to make some southward progress with the American forces in early July. Their southern boundary had changed amazingly little since about three days after our own unit had landed. Admittedly the terrain favoured defence, but the US Army had built up fourteen divisions to the German six. By mid-July Bradley's response had incurred some 40,000 further casualties and achieved very few gains indeed.

If Allied initiative was to be maintained and a major enemy counter-blow prevented, it had to be by the British again. Our 7th and 11th were considered to have recovered from their June engagements, and Guards' Armoured had arrived towards the end of June.

We also knew pitifully little about the enemy's dispositions. Information in the first action had been over-optimistic, and the inference now that 21st Panzer had the only tanks in the immediate area of our proposed attack left us sceptical. We fully expected at the very least that the corridor down which we should proceed would bristle with anti-tank guns and 88 mm dual-purpose guns in their lethal anti-tank role. Our expectations were to be fulfilled.

What we did not know at all was that Rommel, fully expecting us from east of the Orne, had prepared his five defensive zones to a depth of at least ten miles, to include 1st SS as well as the 21st Panzer Division, with formidable reserves in the shape of 2nd Panzer and much of 9th SS moving to an area only five miles from the fifth zone. Additionally 12th SS had been stationed on the flank well east of Troarn to block any threat to Paris or, if appropriate, to fall upon our left rear. Most of our artillery cover would be effective only up to the line of the Caen–Vimont–Lisieux railway, which was barely five miles from starting-point.

If we wondered why British attacks were usually on a front not more than a mile wide, when Soviet ones were increasingly reported covering fronts of over a hundred miles, we also did not know that the German defence in Normandy was 2½ times as thick as what they were opposing at that time to the Red Army, nor that Soviet losses would aggregate 20 million.

Our briefing had told us that no attack could be mounted through Caen itself. Even though the city north of the Orne had been for a week in British and Canadian hands, heavy bomber and naval gunnery attention had left it choked with rubble. These recent weeks of assault must have been an appalling experience for the civilian population.

On 17 July the regiment moved north-east across country to pick up a route to the bridges. Our rear-link tank took in a strand of barbed wire in crossing a hedgerow. I could see the long trail of it catching us up as it wound into the driving-sprocket. The engine note and performance were affected almost at once.

'Driver, halt!'

The squadron left us behind as Albert and I got out to free the strangulation with pick-head, wire-cutters and bare hands. Stanley stood up on my pedestal, blinking into the July sunshine at the surrounding green. Bill listened to the headphones, just in case, aware that the move was being made under strict radio silence. Harry set up the petrol cooker and put on a brew. Then he spotted some large guns at not much over a hundred yards distant. They were firing unhurriedly and there was something different about them. Could he amble over and see what they were at? I nodded. Another strand of wire came out by half a turn.

When Harry came back, we were still struggling and the water was not quite boiled. He stood over us as if his information was more important than what we were sweating at.

'They're Yanks!'

Fair enough, they were the first Americans we had seen since landing. Neither of us so much as glanced at Harry.

Albert's comment was less charitable than mine: 'We could see that from here, you turnip!'

'Yes, but the guns are naval, been brought ashore and set up here to get a bit closer.'

It was the proximity of the sprocket, two-thirds surrounded by projecting tank track, to the hull that made a cramped business of prising out the wire, but we had made notable progress. Harry appreciated our concentration but he had to tell his story. 'They're firing at a bridge over the river at near extreme range, fourteen mile.'

In the mind's eye I guessed this might be the bridge at Thury Harcourt, but there was no time to look at the map.

Albert's response was again less interested: 'Have you got that tea boiled yet?'

Harry had been brought up to persist with the Norfolk soil, or any job he was doing.

'Now why are they firing at that bridge, I ask 'em? They're trying to stop the Tigers we met down beyond Cheux last month from getting back across the River Orne to clobber us when we attack down the far side tomorrow.'

It occurred to me that, if the US Navy knew what we were

going to be doing tomorrow, quite a few other people might have heard too.

Albert was more pragmatic: 'Then you go back, Harry, and wish them Yanks the best of good shooting from me. And if the Tigers don't get back, I'll send 'em a postcard.'

At that moment the water boiled for the tea. Five mugs were filled. Inside ten more minutes the last of the wire was out. Albert wrapped all we had taken out closely round the nearest fence post, so that anyone following in a tank would not have the same thing happen. Harry saw the tools stowed. Then we mounted up and away. All I had to do, instead of following the tank in front, was read the map. On dry, hard fields, Cromwell IVs and VIIs would do over 30 mph in fifth gear, reducing speed only to surmount hedges or other obstacles. We seemed to catch up with A Squadron in no time at all, for they were now part of a longer, slower-moving column, eastbound on a marked route.

The afternoon saw us passing beyond a notice saying 'Dust brings shells' into a dust cloud that emulated the desert – not that any of us had experienced desert dust. It was not just local: it went on and on. Through it we could barely see to follow the tank in front, nor could we see much that we passed, nor the sky above. Those who had goggles put them on; others sought out their mustard-gas eyeshields.

After perhaps twenty minutes it was not shells that started hitting us but a plague of flying insects big as small conkers and at least as hard. The beasties flew with force into our exposed parts, smacking sharply against cheek and forehead. On the tank in front and the tank behind we could just make out the crews parrying and swiping back at the swarm, a blurred picture of desperate combat or near panic.

Albert called me on intercom: might he close his armoured vizor against these hornets and would I guide him from the turret? Was it true you could die if they stung you?

Bill had got down into the turret and closed his hatches

above him. From the depths Stanley, free from dust and marauders, wanted to know what was going on.

Still the tank column kept going.

Another townsman, I found this flying plague a new experience but had a vague idea that hornets were striped. Before I could answer Albert, Harry, who was sitting out on the left 'running-board' with his legs dangling into the co-driver's compartment, untangled his microphone from somewhere at last to beam a Norfolk broadside at Albert.

'They're not 'ornets, you ignorant townie! They're maybugs!'

He had to say it twice more before Albert was reassured. Maybugs in mid-July! Only later came the education that maybugs attack, strip and feed on the foliage of plane and maple trees. The dust prevented our seeing any such trees that might have been in the vicinity, but it was not lost on me that we were driving through a Canadian-held area.

The maybug attack ended, but by the time the dust cloud subsided, it was becoming dusk. In the fading light we became aware of gliders to left and right of our route, monuments to the breathtaking assaults of D-Day almost six weeks ago. The column wound its way to the first bridge, crossed the canal, second bridge, over the river, through more abandoned gliders in the dark, turning south, eventually into a field where Tony was lining us up like in a car-park, packing us in tight.

What an exquisite silence when the last engine switched off! People spoke in whispers. Petrol cookers under the back end only, no lights to show forward, left or right.

Stanley had the shovel; he wanted to do something he had had no chance to do all day.

'Don't go more than ten feet beyond the foremost tank, Stan, or you may be digging up the minefield.'

'Oh, fook!' He went.

Harry could cook in the dark. He heated us tinned stew. Hot and thirsty as the day had been, we enjoyed it, speculating when we might expect the next hot meal. Had the enemy heard us coming in? He must have, could not fail to. Look how jam-packed we were, close as on parade for a general's inspection. If Jerry opened up on us now, with heavies ... We had washed up before the first shell feathered over, bursting at least a field away. Its successor seemed not to bracket us but to be even further off. Perhaps it was meant for the bridges? In the distance some 'moaning Minnies' took off into the night air, their serenade carrying to our ears no more than *pianissimo*. We waited to hear the detonations – except Albert, who made a decision.

'We'll sleep in the Old Girl.'

The driver and co-driver had tolerably comfortable leather-padded seats and back rests. For the turret crew the opportunities to relax were notoriously more limited. I took the shovel from its place to which Stanley had returned it, and began attacking the ground behind the tank. It must have been the hardest subsoil in the beachhead. When I had got down a bare three inches, Harry volunteered to take it on. If the Paras and the Scotties could dig it, a Norfolk farming lad could dig it, he reckoned – until he had been at it for ten minutes. After that he declared that, wherever the Airborne or the Jocks had dug in before, it could not have been just here. He handed me back the shovel and disappeared into the forward hull.

Stan proposed to curl himself round the junction box on the turret floor. Then part of Bill could use the ammunition bins on his side of the gun, while I was invited to 'drape' myself across the gunner's seat, the pedestal and an ammo bin on my side.

Stan explained: 'Better than having to sleep upright.'

I said I should stretch out behind the tank and come inside only if we were shelled, in which case I should try not to wake anyone. Then I had one more go with the shovel, arranging my bedding in the shallow grave, and got in fully dressed, noting that half of me protruded above ground-level.

We had replenished the aluminium-painted drinking jerricans in the turret, and the water cart had departed into the night. I had 'written' a field postcard to my beloved ('I am well. I shall write soon', deleting 'I am wounded' and other inapplicable printed phrases). I thought about us, what little time we had shared so far. It seemed to take a long time for sleep to come, but presumably it did.

My next awareness was of a noise that aroused me fully: tanks. Listening, I reckoned it was the armoured brigade coming into the bridgehead across the same sets of bridges. An enemy shell landed nearer than earlier ones, then another. I got up, made up my bedding. The night air remained warm but I shivered after being wrapped up. Climbing onto the engine covers close to the turret, I swung over as quietly as possible into the commander's cupola, then lowered myself down to try out Stanley's suggested sleeping posture and after some time dozed off.

'What time is it, Skipper?'

Stanley was aware that I was in the tank, whether or not he had heard me come in – how long ago was that? I looked at my watch, the figures glowing green in the dark of the interior.

'Three o'clock, Stan. Are you all right down there?'

'Thanks, yes.'

Silence again. The watch dial still glowed before me. I thought I saw beyond it to the face of her who had given it me. Perhaps she had wakened too at that moment. I contemplated the incredible serenity with which I knew she could sleep. I acknowledged that, whereas I was in danger for only a few days at a time – and then just relaxed in the green summer Normandy countryside for longer periods, she could think I was at risk continually. How much might that mar her serenity, her ordinarily profound sleep?

About 5 a.m. the Pathfinders were heard. I shifted my position for the hundredth time, hoisted myself upright to park on the cupola rim. The sticky warmth of the tank interior contrasted with the cleanliness of the pre-dawn air. If I shivered now, the exchange was still welcome.

As the multiples of four engines came closer, other tank hatches clanked open, crews stirred. Harry dived under the rear end with his screened cooker to prepare the morning ambrosia. Soon we were sipping at it from our seats in the pit stalls.

While dark remained, the flak bursts scintillated viciously, as they must have for countless night-bomber incursions over Europe, all round the barely visible droning black cargo-heavy fuselages. Flares launched to illuminate ground targets seemed only to confuse the sky picture seen from below. At an early stage we could occasionally glimpse festoons of tinsel foil twisting down to disrupt defensive detection systems.

As the sky lightened, we began to identify individual aircraft, to witness the pulling power in each of four Rolls-Royce engines, knowing that just one such engine powered a Spitfire or our Cromwell tank.

Some flashes where bombs landed preceded by several seconds the muffled sounds of detonation. There was no telling whether the immense destruction was on target; all we knew was that nothing landed anywhere near us.

The operation continued as inexorably as the time it takes for a thousand bombers to have their turn over a limited target area. From where we were, only one Lancaster appeared to be hit. It moved out of formation with a black smoke trail, flames spreading to furnace intensity. What could survive in that heat? Then parachutes appeared near the wake of the stricken craft – two, three, four ... then no more, although the crew was eight?

One 'chute was itself on fire. The plane went into a dive. We thought we heard the whining crescendo of it above all the other noises. The frame burst vividly into the ground well behind enemy lines. In the packed bridgehead, tank crews trying intensely to keep track of the baled-out airmen were already identifying with the same desperate act by which, from a few feet above ground, many of them would soon be escaping their own blazing vehicles.

When the RAF completed, the USAAF began, in semi-daylight, gunning up the trail the tanks must follow, to the hills of the Bourgebus ridge, aiming to treat the fortified villages in our path to the non-cratering effect of high-fragmentation bombing. We watched their lower-altitude tails clearing our bereted heads and dusting away south and slightly west to annihilate opposition until all we had to do was drive. Would it be like that?

As the last of the Havocs and Marauders skated into the distance, the artillery programme took over, most guns firing from the far side of the River Orne. Two more divisions of armour would need to be brought across the bridges before the guns could be repositioned on the ground about to be gained.

Tank engines started and warmed from 0730. At full strength to begin the advance, the regiment mustered sixty-one Cromwell tanks. In a quarter of an hour we were moving to the taped exits through our own minefields, in nominal daylight still psychologically sunless and dim. Headphones rustled, radios already netted.

Bill and I, with our heads out of the top as we followed Mac and Tony through a gap, were reminded by the sight of a tank disabled at the very edge of the tape, that C Squadron had preceded us. They were to support the infantry brigade into Cuverville, then they or B into Demouville, while we in A Squadron watched the divisional right flank, with orders to neutralize any opposition materializing from the Caen factory suburb of Colombelles.

We gave the disabled tank a wide berth. One of its tracks had been parted by an unmarked mine. Its commander, Lieutenant Bromhead, nicknamed 'Blue', was down beside his vehicle with a sledgehammer, working to repair the damage. He would have to winch in some of the track from where it lay neatly in rear of the point at which its parent had halted. On the hull he carried some spare links to replace the ones blown. He looked up as we passed and wrinkled his nose at me in a way characteristic of the short time I had known him. Wielding a sledgehammer had affinities with putting the shot, throwing discus or hammer, whereas 'Blue's' enthusiasm was for rugby football.

Clear of the mines, A Squadron deployed out to the right, the five troops of three in a skeleton starfish about the diamond four of squadron HQ, nineteen tanks in all. We had no thin-skinned AA tank in this operation.

Now we used binoculars to probe the mist and smoke engulfing Colombelles for signs of opposition to neutralize. The Canadians were scheduled to clear the suburb, so we could not shoot to draw fire. It was impossible to tell what was happening. As soon as Mac reckoned the squadron had reached a position from which it could do its job, he stopped, and the squadron conformed. All sat looking at the undecipherable, the impenetrable, the still smouldering area. That any opposition had been half-buried and left disoriented by the RAF raid seemed probable. If the effect was as cratered as Caen north of the river had been, the Canadians might be expected to make slow work of clearing through.

On regimental net the colonel instructed me to report when we were in position. I complied at once: 'In position. Over.'

Then he had to know just what that position was. I took a guess from the map, there being no landmarks by which to double-check, encoded the grid reference into letters and sent the result.

'Can you see any opposition yet? Over.'

'Not yet. Too much smoke and mist. Over.'

An enemy shell landed just beyond squadron HQ, bursting menacingly but away from us towards the rear. I reported it to regiment, believing it came not from the area we were watching but from the high ground to the south. A second shell burst between that high ground and squadron HQ. They had bracketed us.

I waved at the commanders of the other three tanks and ordered Albert to start up and move us one hundred yards further east. Our vehicle moved promptly, Tony Venner's and the HQ sergeant's conforming. Only Big Mac's remained immobile, the squadron commander oblivious to all but where his eyes just above the cupola ring searched through binoculars into the silent suburb.

Instead of firing for effect, the enemy fired one more shot only. It landed right beside Mac's tank, seeming to rock it, but even this did not move him.

Several uncharted factory chimneys survived to probe above the Colombelles murk like minarets. I discussed with the crew whether an enemy observation post was likely to be concealed at the top of one of them. They thought the chimneys too precarious, such a long way to climb even if there were internal ladders all the way. The roof of a factory building was a more likely spot, but from our position most of these were more obscure than the chimneys. Some of them were burning. If we shelled the ones that looked more intact, we might damage some Canadians. We had heard nothing of any liaison arrangement on this flank.

To our left, squadron after squeaking squadron of Shermans drove flat out for the armoured brigade objectives to the south, disappearing into dusty obscurity. The corridor was the nearest thing to an open plain to be found in Normandy, but it was picketed by the orchard and other tree clumps of the villages which the enemy had fortified, beginning on our left frontal view with Cuverville and Demouville, which the Shermans left on their right as they bypassed both, responsibility for capture having been allocated to the infantry brigade.

Bren-gun carriers were careering across the open ground towards the first of these villages now, closer to us than the Shermans had been. The enemy battery that had bracketed squadron HQ turned its attention to the larger, if moving, target of the infantry assault, scoring a direct hit on a carrier at full speed. A thick black smoke column rose vertically to the windless sky, pyre of carrier and crew, making an aiming mark for further salvoes.

The regimental net began to hear about Cuverville, and support to the infantry now arrived there. C Squadron had also heard from the crew of 'Blue's' tank back in the mine gap, that they were hammering in the final link when enemy shelling straddled them. The lieutenant, hit in the leg, had been evacuated, ready to be flown back to the UK. A leg: what would that do for his rugby?

The sun made itself felt. Harry asked if he could get out and brew up some tea at the back of the tank. Before I could answer (and I noted that no other tanks had crews outside the hulls), the long-range enemy guns turned their attention to us again. Again three tanks of HQ moved position, while Big Mac's remained immovable. Was our commander setting a brave example or was he oblivious to what was going on around him as he concentrated on control of five troops, stationary and observing an invisible and perhaps non-existent opposition? I had to remind myself that it was his first time as a squadron commander in action. He had been into action in a tank one more time than I had – which was no times at all, so that whatever my personal feelings about him I ought not to be prematurely critical. His was a sizeable responsibility and I was there to help, not to carp.

It was when the CO wanted information from the squadron commander's own lips that contacting the latter was to prove specially difficult. Bill must have guessed this might be so from his longer knowledge of personalities in the regiment. He had made an arrangement with Big Mac's radio-operator that when I needed to speak to Mac on the short-range 'B' set, Bill or I would wave to attract the operator's attention and then grasp the corrugated rubber mounting of our 'B' set aerial.

The moment came for putting this simple arrangement to the test when the colonel, tired of hearing me say we could still see no opposition in the suburbs, asked me to get squadron commander to 'flick' to regimental net for a direct conversation with RHQ. I acknowledged the CO with a 'Wilco. Out' (standard response for 'Will comply') and looked towards Mac's tank, some fifty yards distant.

Because of the intermittent shelling, the operator had got his head down inside. Only the top of Mac's beret was visible on his side, as he looked either at the three troops in front or at Colombelles, and never at us. Eventually it was Tony, the second-in-command, who saw my gesticulations and waved to acknowledge. He then used the squadron net on his 'A' set to tell Mac I was trying to reach him on 'B'.

Once the message was passed and I heard Mac tell the

colonel nothing more than I had been able to, I stood down off the pedestal, turned about to half-fill everyone's mug from the 'silver' jerricans stowed between radio and grenade box, then passed them round. The day continued to warm up. With the ration of drinking-water, Harry conceded to await a more favourable opportunity for getting out to make tea. He buttered us all some hardtack, sliced the bully beef and handed it round.

C Squadron announced the destruction of two enemy self-propelled 105 mm guns (standard field guns mounted on a tank hull). Cuverville was reported clear by about 10 a.m. The brigade and its support would press on to take Demouville.

I wondered how 3 Div. was progressing against the tree-covered slopes on the left of the corridor. It had looked dark and foreboding as we drove out to our position on the right, almost as if I could feel the forward scouts of the invisible 12th SS there, waiting at the right psychological moment to fall upon our left rear.

No news yet either of the armoured brigade, long since disappeared over the first railway line (the east–west Caen–Troarn, running immediately south of Demouville), and for all we knew beyond the second line as well. The first wave of armour had moved behind a rolling barrage put down by field artillery and keeping perhaps a hundred yards ahead of it. The barrage had to stop this side of the second railway, the Caen–Vimont–Mezidon–Lisieux and eventually Paris line, simply because that was the limit of field-gun range.

After several more squadron HQ moves to foil the enemy gunners and several more attempts to get answers from Mac to a series of questions put by colonel or adjutant, my normally even temper was evidently fraying.

'Tell you what,' Bill said as he took another mug of barely cool water from me, 'the Old Girl is stuffed tight with free cigarettes. Why don't you join the rest of us and become a smoker?'

I accepted a tin of fifty, pierced the foil with the triangular metal blade provided in the lid, hearing the air hiss in, twisted the lid full circle, took out and lighted my first cigarette since teenage, along with Bill's umpteenth. By now the middle day was really hot, and over those distant hills to the south the earlier mist had been replaced by an equally obscure heat haze. My attempts through binoculars to spot their guns firing – they were probably concealed by a fold in the ground anyway – now increasingly risked catching the blinding sunlight.

Just as a long lull between shell arrivals had started up Harry's plea again to get out and brew up, regiment ordered us forward to support the armoured brigade, still with a right-flank responsibility. I struggled once more to engage Mac's attention, caught his operator's and conveyed the order on 'B' set. As I switched back to 'A', another squadron was reporting several of its tanks being boarded by Panzer grenadiers, who just swarmed up out of the standing corn in which the squadron had been unwise enough to become stationary, attacking the turrets with machine-pistols and egg grenades. Crews had closed down hatches and used both radio sets to exhort neighbours to machine-gun them clear. One radio-operator had had a lobbed grenade lodge in his neckerchief and barely managed to dispose of it before it burst.

'Did you get the map reference of that lot?' I asked Bill, thinking it a good area to steer A Squadron clear of, but he shook his head. We were all moving. Big Mac was leading us south to carry out the order.

Someone at RHQ chose the moment of the report of being boarded by the enemy to ask a question. B Squadron tanks had been fitted with strips of rubber composite to defeat the use of magnetic mines. The question asked of the closed-down squadron under attack was: 'Any sign of the use of magnetic mines? Over.'

'God knows when we'll get a brew-up now!' Harry set a good example of having no inhibitions over self-expression in our tank.

'So long as it's not us as gets brewed up, young 'Arry!' Stanley was waking up after a morning of inactivity.

''Ere, where was it them Jerries climbed up on the tanks?' Albert had been thinking about the report he had heard by induction from 'A' set into the intercom.

'I didn't hear where. We'd just better avoid stopping still in the cornfields.'

I quite expected Harry to give us a whimsical lecture on the difference between wheat, barley and maize fields, and popular misuse of the word 'corn', but he did not. As we moved nearer to the real battlefield, every one of us was sucking hard at a cigarette.

It was a fairly open corridor as we skirted Cuverville. Nothing fired at us while we were on the move, that we noticed. Then we were abreast of Demouville, and our approach to the railway obstacles and other cover spoiled our earlier view of the distant, haze-covered hills that remained the divisional objective.

Beyond Demouville and across the Caen–Troarn railway, Mac shunted a couple of troops to the front and set them looking for a way past the main line joining Caen to Vimont and Mezidon. There was also a railway emanating from Colombelles that turned south, crossing over the other two lines to climb into the hazy high ground. This third line divided Bourgebus from Hubert Folie and disappeared into the upper distance in the direction of Bretteville-sur-Laize. This was the most embankmented line of them all. Its immediate military potential was to give cover to troops on either side of it from the fire of forces on the other. As we were to find, however, the enemy had both sides raked by fire most of the time, certainly at points beyond the Caen–Vimont line, so that any advantages from the dividing embankment were at best intermittent.

On the way down, a garbled report on regimental net implied that B Squadron had preceded us beyond the Caen–Vimont line, where it had lost two tanks to enemy self-propelled guns concealed in the Cormelles factory area, which was on the right of the embankmented north–south railway, on the flank which was becoming our squadron's responsibility in this more forward area. B had used smoke to get the rest of its tanks clear, and they were now on the left of the embankmented line and straddling the Caen–Vimont, to support the armoured units that had gone forward on that side.

The canny Mac now directed our squadron through a small bridgeway or mini-tunnel under the embankmented line, so as to be on the right (west) side of it but still just short of the Caen–Vimont. Hopefully we should be able this way to make contact with the right forward armoured regiment of the brigade. Once through the hole, Big Mac deployed his troops forward up the slope to where clumps of trees punctuated further view. From there they could see a number of Shermans apparently empty or on fire, but no manned tanks to communicate with.

How significant was this? Where was the nucleus of the regiment in front? How drastic had its losses been? Where was Tac Brigade?

What was fact in the next period was that, although RHQ on radio asked not only B but C Squadron (now released from the infantry brigade because Demouville also had been cleared) how their southward probing was progressing, it made no attempt to shift us from our tight new position facing up a slope to the half-right, a position from which troops could shoot at the bellies of any enemy tanks crossing the Caen–Vimont line from south to north.

All was quiet enough here at the moment, all engines switched off for a rest. Harry asked if he could brew up underneath the back end. I said he had better be alert to get back in but he might have a try. I concentrated on a message from RHQ.

Squadron HQ was half-way up the initial slope. We had not been there long, and I had persisted with another effort to communicate with Mac on 'B' set, when a fusillade of high-velocity armour-piercing shot (at once reminding me of the counter-attack last month upon Hill 112) began whizzing over and among us, seeming to come from the left or left front. A hundred yards behind us the railway embankment offered the obvious cover.

'Driver, start up, reverse!!'

Albert instantly buttoned to turn the engine over and over until all twelve cylinders sprang into life. Other Cromwells were doing the same. As he crammed the gear lever into reverse, getting it in first time by flicking a tiller bar which bodily jerked the whole tank several inches right and back again, Albert freed a hand to press the prestle switch on his microphone and say, as he let in the clutch and the tank rolled astern, 'Is Harry clear?' He got to me.

'Driver, halt!!'

I had forgotten Harry. How could I? I threw off my headphones and thrust myself up out of the cupola towards the world of flying metal. Harry lumbered along beside the left of the tank, swung his cooker like a small suitcase onto the running-board and clambered into the co-driver's hatch. He looked far from squashed flat.

Third and fourth salvoes of AP (armour-piercing shot) zinged all round. I dropped back inside, cramming on headphones and breathing determinedly into the microphone.

'Driver, reverse.' My real breathlessness reasserted itself, still on intercom. 'Harry, I forgot you. Will you ever forgive me?'

Harry sounded not even ruffled, just his usual self: 'Lord bless you, Skipper! I 'eard the engine start and felt the gear go in when she rocked. I knew it was an emergency and I doused the cooker, which is safe and sound here with me. With the tank moving, I just couldn't reach the dixie with the water, which was pretty warm, so we've lost that. I'm sorry.'

'Are you all right?'

'I'm fine. With the Old Girl rolling back, it was me or the dixie, and I won.'

On 'A' set, B Squadron was reporting a full-scale counter-attack down the south side of the Caen–Vimont line, from the villages of Four and Frénouville, with Panther tanks demonstrating the remarkable effectiveness of their high-velocity 75 mm guns. I imagined B Squadron sharing the experience with the bulk of the left-flank armoured regiment of Shermans, one in four equipped with seventeen-pounder guns that could kill Panthers. None of us had any idea how substantially the numbers of the Shermans had already been reduced, first by anti-tank batteries at Cagny and then by Panther and self-propelled gunfire from the ridge ahead. Now B Squadron commander was reported wounded in the mouth, and there were other casualties.

A Squadron HQ subsided into the protection of the embankment. The forward troops had crept into the higher tree clumps for cover from view. There we all waited for the outcome of the onslaught down the other side of the main railway line, and for whatever might happen next.

I was wondering two things: why was our division not using rocket-firing aircraft to break up the Panther counter-attack, and when were we going to see any sign of the other two armoured divisions?

The answer to the first was that the RAF LO this time had been mounted in a tank to keep up with the armoured regiments. His tank had been knocked out, putting 'ground control' out of action. Deprived of this explanation at the time, we only knew we saw no aircraft.

The second question, 'when', was indeed a matter of time. Leading elements of Guards Armoured had been temporarily diverted by tanks of the 21st Panzer Division, some of which they knocked out. Then they were engaged by the 88 mm guns of Tigers surviving from the morning's flank bombing. The Tigers shot up the left of the British corridor from positions near Emieville, and the Guards in this, their first action, took them on.

It must have been near to 4 p.m. when the counter-attack on B Squadron positions had eased off and I felt reckless enough to stand on turret top to look east over the railway embankment, that I could see some of their dark grey-painted Shermans and Fireflies on the move between us and the general area of Cagny. Their turrets bore the sign of an eye in a shield. Cagny itself was to be overrun by the Guards later in the day, but their progress towards Vimont would be opposed from every village on the way and by the Panthers that had withdrawn in that direction. As I descended again into the turret, B Squadron was reporting to regiment a similar sighting of our dark grey neighbours.

The sun was still hot. Drinking-water was low in two out of three jerricans because we had been trickling it out all day. We ate more canned beef and biscuit. All smoked incessantly. In the lee of the embankment it seemed safe to get out to water the weeds only very occasionally, when it became an urgent necessity.

Later, while the day cooled, RHQ called for supply requirements. The echelon was organized in lorry-loads of either petrol, ammunition, food or other stores, but there was also provision for calling up a mixed load combining all three. I spoke to Tony on 'B' set. As second-in-command, the decision was his. We agreed that, while we all needed petrol and food, squadron usage of ammunition had been minimal. The day was by no means over but he reckoned that our best bet was a mixed load, and this I ordered.

Putting down the headphones, I climbed up again on turret top and looked across the railway at the corridor to our left. I was in time to see two Cromwells and a Sherman Firefly, well spaced, moving unhurriedly southward. The Firefly's seventeen-pounder was not pointing naïvely forward but half-left across the line of advance of the troop. The movement conveyed to me a sense of control and co-ordination, with each tank relating to the others and alert for targets.

Although all three were moving, any one could quickly halt and sustain supporting fire while the other two spurted for whatever cover might be available. Their whole operation contrasted with the one which had seemed to characterize the earlier part of our day, that of whole squadrons charging along in formation or column, when anti-tank fire from concealed guns could kill off virtually every tank inside two minutes.

The turrets of the newcomers carried one five-blanket

bedroll slung behind instead of folded blankets being stowed in the bins. It made me wonder what they, perhaps like George Bernard Shaw's chocolate soldier, carried in their bins. When the troop passed beyond me, closing with the Caen–Vimont railway, my binoculars magnified the collection of frying-pans, sliced half-jerricans and other substantial culinary impedimenta swinging from hooks and wires along the rear hull below the exhaust cowling.

Now I could read the insignia – of course, the red jerboa of 7th Armoured, the Desert Rats. So some of them were clear of the Orne bridges at last, filtering down ready to restore the momentum of the British assault on the morrow, meanwhile not presenting any concentrated targets to Panther or dual-purpose 88 mm. Experience from Cairo to Naples must count for something. As the troop drew near the main railway line, I swung my binoculars back to search the direction from which they had come. There was the next troop just into view, same pace. My watch said six.

Harry brewed tea, having found the dixie up in the field. The track had missed it. He forecast mulligatawny soup for supper. Inside some three more hours, with nothing too significant happening, we were beginning to feel that, if the main forward movement had stopped, at least with the arrival of Guards and some of 7th we could hang on to what we had gained, perhaps make better progress next day.

All of a sudden, an alert! Regimental net reported Tiger tanks emerging from the southern suburbs of Caen itself, driving at present approximately in the direction of our squadron.

We got Harry back into the tank. Squadron HQ moved up the slope again, ready to thicken any salvoes the troops might be in a position to deliver. There was still some daylight left. Albert asked me on intercom what was so special about Tigers. He knew but he must have wanted my version.

'Fifty-six tons to our twenty-eight. At least double the

thickness of our frontal armour. Their 88 mm gun will penetrate anything the Allies have got, and at a range of over a mile.'

'So what do we do?'

'If they keep coming this way, I hope we hold our fire until they present us with a belly target coming over the brow. What's left of the sun should be behind them but it's not in our eyes. Perhaps they won't see us until we perforate them.' I wanted to believe it.

Gunfire broke out somewhere in front.

'Stand by!!'

The sounds were of a two-way duel, but who was firing on our side? C Squadron was somewhere on our right. Each time they had broken cover to advance across the open during the late afternoon, a hail of fire had sent them back to ground. Perhaps now they could see something to shoot at. But if it were C Squadron, why was I hearing no reports on regimental net? Then again, it could be a nucleus of the Sherman regiment we had failed to locate.

We stayed tense until half-dark, when the firing petered out. It had not reached us, and yet we were ignorant of its conclusion. Mac's clever positioning of us just north of the main line had undoubtedly protected us from a great deal of trouble. Apparently it also impaired our contact with neighbours. Perhaps the Tigers had turned south to join the Panthers on the ridge?

Regiment ordered withdrawal of the squadron through the railway arch, to harbour in the open on the far side, about 300 yards into the corridor. The word was passed and Mac conducted us all back. In darkness we lined up at the appointed spot, in a single line nose to tail, facing slightly east of south.

While I was concerned about where the Tigers had gone and what we might hear from them in the morning, Harry was full of speculation about where they had come from. If they had appeared so late in the day south of the river, were they not the very ones the regiment had faced south-west of Cheux last month? He concluded that, for all the use the American naval gunners had been in shelling that distant river bridge, they might as well have stayed on their battleship. He might have been right, but as we had no news of Canadian progress in clearing the southern suburbs, there was no knowing whether the Tigers had been there all the time, perhaps just recovered from the morning's air bombardment and ordered to pull out before dusk to fight again from higher ground tomorrow.

For the night we were so much out in the open that those on turret watch ought to spot an infantry incursion before it could close with the line of tanks, but that was all the protection we appeared to have. Perhaps, in allocating the spot, RHQ knew that the motor battalion was dug in at nearby Grentheville, but we did not.

To this night location the water cart and our mixed load suddenly appeared out of the gloom. We all turned to, seizing jerricans across the lowered tailboard, carrying them down the line of tanks to pass up to drivers standing on engine covers, ready to pour the petrol into the insatiable fillers. Harry and Stan carried and checked our crew's share of the ration pack. Bill and I made sure we replenished from the cart our three water jerricans, raising them to turret top, lowering into position, fastening the clamp. In the process Bill sent my fifty-cigarette tin skidding against the grenade box.

Once the guard arrangements had been made, I could afford to remember how tired I was. After last night's kind of rest it had been a long day of inactive watching, on tenterhooks. Now Bill and I were to take the final turret watch before dawn stand-to. Before then, it would be another short night of sleep inside.

Perhaps it was as well we had so little information about the general situation. The facts might have inhibited even the amount of sleep we did achieve. Our division, the Bull, had lost around half its tank strength of perhaps 250. In the hours of dark, the Luftwaffe was bombing by flarelight the bridges area as replacements and crews struggled forward and further losses were incurred. Our A Squadron must have been the only one in the division to remain complete and unscathed. The logic of that was that we should play a leading part in the events of the morrow.

The Oxford tactical course taught that a German counter-attack could be counted upon as soon as you made a gain of any significance. As sleep claimed me now, I reflected that I had not really been surprised by today's Panther and Tiger sallies, but again I knew nothing of the realities of the enemy situation from which they had produced the resilient resistance that we in A Squadron had heard rather than seen.

In fact, an infantry division newly arrived from the South of France had relieved the 1st SS Panzer Division from its front-line commitment astride the River Orne further south and west. Having just been refitted before we first encountered it near Hill 112 at the end of last month, this forceful veteran of the Eastern Front had been moved up on the 18th, the morning of our attack, to the very high ground we were intended to reach. There its Panthers and mobile assault guns had picked ridge positions from which to take heavy toll of the Shermans of the armoured brigade advancing uphill over open ground towards the fortified villages of Bras, Hubert Folie and Soliers. Once the Cromwells of B Squadron had crossed the main railway line, some of the Panthers had advanced from cover to cover – to avoid air surveillance – until they could mount the counter-attack from Four and Frenouville against B and the surviving Shermans.

1st SS was not the only formation being magnetized to stem the British attack. The 2nd Panzer Division, recently earmarked to take care of the St-Lô sector in depth, had moved east of the Orne to block our path to Falaise. The 116th Panzer Division, recently released from the German 15th Army guarding Calais and the Somme, on the move from Amiens to an area west of St-Lô, was now diverted to stop off south of Caen. So our present assault was to be contained by 5½ Panzer divisions, leaving 1½ to watch the British west of the Orne, and only two opposite the Americans. Was it coincidence that on the 18th also US forces at last captured St-Lô?

Through June crops, Churchills supported the Scotsmen

An unending quest for snipers was just one recognition of the enemy's tenacity

Wheeled seventeen-pounder anti-tank guns moving up

Shermans passing a knocked-out Tiger

The RAF could stand a Tiger on its head

Captured intact 31 July, under traffic control 2 August: queuing for the one Souleuvre bridge (behind camera)

Across the River Orne into the narrow bridgehead

Assault by three armoured divisions meant one at a time on 18 July: some crews ready for 'off'

Still loaded: 'Moaning Minnie' rockets in a captured six-barrelled mortar

Into Vassy, mid-August: a 2nd Northamptonshire Yeomanry Cromwell

Caen in July, impassably choked with rubble

. . . Fair warning, but in mid-July dust was unavoidable

Third go, 30 July: Montgomery switched British armour to push southward on the left of American XIX Corps

6 An Elastic Day

I was wakened from a sleep curled round the junction box to take final turn on guard. Bill and I stood with head and shoulders above our respective hatches and peered into the surrounding darkness. The only sounds were of Stanley settling down in the bottom of the turret where I had been, and of his watch partner from another tank regaining his own vehicle for at most two hours' sleep.

July nights are longer than June ones. The present example was quite warm. After barely four hours' rest the two of us made an effort to become and remain alert. If either spoke – and then only in an undertone, it was as much as anything to make sure we were still awake.

'D'you reckon we're winning?' Bill asked once.

I waffled: 'We made four or five miles yesterday, after the bombing. Today could be slower going, probably. May depend how much artillery we've been able to bring across the river during the night, if any.'

'But do you reckon we're winning the war? I mean it's over a month since we landed, and they seem to stem us up every time we try to break out.'

I answered sleepily. Even when Britain faced invasion, I had had no doubt we should win. I should just like to survive to see it. Bill agreed, hoped our crew would come through. We must do our best, I nodded sombrely, missing my proper sleep.

When at last the sky began to lighten, we woke others for stand-to. Harry screened the cooker under the back of the tank, brewed tea. We sipped at it gratefully, hot, tin-creamy and sweet.

A high-velocity gun sounded from somewhere along the distant high ground – vaguely visible again because we were clear of the embankment – and a shot thudded into the turf beside our line of Cromwells. Then a second one! I could barely discern the outline of the ridge above and far beyond the railway. The 88 mm must have a twilight gunsight.

'Start up!'

Big Mac was awake. Buttons were pressed, turning the engines over and over and over until they fired, each with a healthy roar and short-lived exhaust flames, converted by the cowlings from up to down, and great puffs of initial smoke that insisted on rising slowly.

As the hostile gunners persisted, Mac ignored the makers' injunction to warm engines before moving off. His tank's clutch was slipped and the twenty-eight tons eased forward to lead us out in a wide circle left, then down the slope into the lee of the north–south railway embankment. Incredibly enough, in the whole cumbersome manoeuvre not one tank was hit.

Radios on, Bill checked the regimental net on the way, answering the morning call. A Squadron went back through the hole in the embankment and took up its positions of the day before on the slope beyond. It was about half an hour after the time the German guns took potshots at us that the light improved sufficiently for Stanley to report his telescope functional.

After the experience of yesterday, B Squadron was to be in reserve. C Squadron came by to the right to reconnoitre forward onto the open slope towards Bras and Hubert Folie again. Their very first appearance attracted withering fire from both villages and the ridge between – perhaps even more vigorous than the day before, and they were prudently pulled back, swinging west instead, to explore the Cormelles factory area, from which B Squadron had come under fire the previous day.

This morning C Squadron found Cormelles clear of enemy, except for one or two self-propelled guns which withdrew as they approached. They promptly occupied the factory area and also some woods just south of it. This made a base from which the regiment could try a fresh assault on the ridge from the west side. Preparations took RHQ time to complete and translate into summonses to squadrons to move first to the new base area. In A Squadron Harry took advantage of the hiatus to produce an appetizing late breakfast for the rear-link crew.

The enemy situation was that 1st SS had relieved an exhausted 21st Panzer Division during the night, taking over infantry positions and the garrisoning of the fortified villages. It was probably their wide-awake enterprise in the half-light just after dawn that had pumped long-range AP into our stand-to.

Now C Squadron reported seeing Panzer grenadiers digging in at exemplary speed on a slope between Cormelles and Bras. C had been shelling them but they had ostensibly disappeared below ground with the despatch of crabs into sand. Their camouflage was remarkable.

From assembly area to start line – not exactly defined but intended to be 'turret down' (i.e. tanks out of sight) from the SS defenders of Bras – was perhaps a thousand yards, across open country, part cereal and part uncut grass. A Squadron was on the left, C right, B still initially in reserve at the base area.

We moved forward as ordered at a walking pace consistent with supporting an infantry attack. The reason for this pace was not explained, and there was no infantry with us. Our line of approach up a partly convex slope looked from the map to keep us out of sight from Bras itself, but the intervening fields could conceal infantry and anti-tank gun positions, and the whole operation out in the open would be under observation from enemy artillery-spotters on higher ground further south along the ridge, as well as initially from places along the river valley to the west, where the Canadians had not yet reached the village of Ifs.

I wondered at the time why we were driving so slowly. Was it to avoid running on a minefield? I remember thinking how, between the wars, an under-financed British tank-development programme had seemed undecided between the infantry tank concept of World War I and the long-range cruiser for Blitzkrieg excursions (which the enemy had then put into practice) and tried to evolve both.

I might have reflected that the regiment's present approach-line was not so very far away from the points at which C Squadron had more than once been turned back by a hail of anti-tank fire.

As the advance began, a stream of messages began to flow in from regimental net, involving decoding of map and other references and marking-up in chinagraph pencil the sheet of talc secured over my map. As we were grinding through crops, I stepped down into the turret to concentrate, having first given Albert a distant aiming-mark to drive steadily towards. He was at liberty to close his armoured vizor if enemy infantry appeared or if we were shot at.

From my first day with the tank, Albert had shown concern that I should not suffer the fate of his previous commander. ('Whatever you do, Skipper, keep out of the airbursts!') He had rigged on my cupola a convex driving-mirror on a long metal arm, a farewell present from Nobby when I moved from RHQ. By unfastening the bolt on the cupola I could swivel it, watching the mirror from inside the turret, to see whether the engine plates of the tank were swarming with Panzer grenadiers and to detect other things of interest in our immediate vicinity, such as a trench with bazooka men. It was all great stuff in theory. While I was 'below' to do my decoding and map-marking (which proved to contain nothing of much significance), I occasionally swivelled the cupola and cricked my neck to use the mirror from more than one angle, but noticed nothing alarming.

Acknowledging what I hoped was the final message, I stepped on the pedestal and took a quick glance at our environment. There were no Panzer grenadiers, no one was shooting at anyone, but the rear-link tank was proceeding in glorious isolation some 200 yards in front of the squadron! I switched to intercom and informed my companions, deciding on the simple course of driving a half-circle left to re-enter the squadron line through any space that should present, then to swing about again and rejoin SHQ.

Stanley voiced an apprehension he was probably not alone in feeling: 'I 'ope none of them sleepy boogers don't mistake us for a Tiger.'

'More like they'll say, "What's our rear link up to this time?" '

It was brilliant sunshine but there were few heads above hatches, and everyone would be tense. I told Stan to keep our gun pointing towards a clump of bushes that was in the general direction of the enemy. I had to face-about on the pedestal to watch Albert find a gap between tanks without problems. I waved reassuringly, I hoped nonchalantly, to the squadron line as we approached it. No one waved back.

Then we were through, turning to come up with squadron HQ at the very moment the squadron halted, after which you could have counted ten before the artillery concentration hit us. Great spurts of earth leapt up all round. Our tank rocked and rocked again. Albert's armoured vizor clanged to. Then he yelled at me on intercom.

'Get your 'ead down, Skipper!'

I already had.

I reported to regiment that we had halted at 'turret-down' and were being 'stonked' by what seemed like mediums. Could regiment arrange counter-battery fire?

Ignoring my bright suggestion, the adjutant distinctly said: 'Orders. Proceed slowly and with caution towards objective, watching out for friends on the left. And report. Out.'

This order had to be conveyed to squadron commander to implement it. The concentration continued. I tried 'B' set several times. No reply.

The stonk abated. Head out, I could see Mac's tank in front and slightly right of ours, the second-in-command's tank on its immediate left, unnaturally close alongside.

'We're going up next to Major Mac's tank on his right. I'm going to jump across and pass him the order direct. Driver, advance, right and left. Don't hit him and don't give me too far to jump. Bill, come up ready to guide Albert.'

Albert let in the clutch. The Cromwell surged forward in first gear, slewing right, then left onto an accurate line of approach.

'Bill, take control until I'm back. Stan, watch I don't knock you for six if I have to come back fast. Albert, that's just right. Driver, halt!'

My headphones and mike were on turret top. I was out beside it. I jumped across to the other tank, one metal-studded boot on a thin sloped bin lid, the other on an engine plate behind Mac's turret. Both boots slid until one was stopped by the turret's vertical side. I grabbed the operator's rear hatch. We had stability! What else did we have?

Captain Tony Venner was already standing on the opposite side of Mac's turret. His usual friendly grin welcomed me as if this were an everyday occurrence, but I sensed there was a more serious glint in his eye. He nodded at the turret. Below hatches Big Mac, affecting to concentrate on his map, was dabbing with a bloodstained pocket handkerchief at a point behind and below his right ear. His headphones rested perilously forward, rucking his ordinarily smoothed-down hair and the beret that perched on it.

'Shell splinter, sir!' Mac's operator was aware of the two captains peering in.

Tony was more to the point: 'Trouble is, he's gone bloody deaf!'

The operator nudged his commander, pointing up at me. Looking up, Mac caught the expression of concern on my face.

'It's nothing, Keith. I'm all right. What does the colonel want?'

We are told that the British are brought up to shout at

anyone who is deaf or foreign. I shouted into the turret: 'Proceed slowly towards objective, with caution. Watch out for friends on the left. And report.'

Big Mac shook his head; he had not got it. The operator pulled one of his own headphones aside to hear the order. As I was about to try again, louder, he made an offer: 'Don't worry, sir. I'll write it down for him.' He did so, repeating the order aloud, getting it right. I looked at Tony, who was busting to speak.

'I've offered to take over the squadron and send him back. He ignores me. We may have to clobber him if he doesn't lose enough blood and pass out. If he's that deaf on radio, we're risking the squadron.'

I nodded. Mac was reading the message, acknowledging comprehension at me, switching to 'A' set, grasping his microphone to speak to the five troops.

'What the hell does that mean, "friends on the left"?'

The question, from Tony, was the signal for the first three shells of the next stonk arriving among us. Tony and I leapt for our respective tanks.

'Look out, Stanley!'

Through-vaulting two-handed over my turret, I plummeted down past the cupola as cascades of earth reared up and explosions hammered at the eardrums. Stan was too slow in moving back onto his gunner's stool. One of my boots landed on his shoulder, the other removed his beret onto the turret floor. He moaned with pain and I stood pressing myself into the back of the turret while he recovered headgear, headphones and dignity onto his stool.

'Driver, advance, ease right, clear of the major!'

Albert complied, although he was still closed down, and I stepped on and off the pedestal several times in the next minutes to see if he needed guiding. At the first look I saw that the major was away clear and we had space in front for some way. Whether we eventually drove out of the concentration or whether the enemy guns just completed their firing programme I was scarcely aware as we focused on the move to our objective.

Tanks surmounted the gentle convex slope until there in front of us was the wooded area that was Bras. If we could see the village, its defenders could see us.

Big Mac had been speaking into his microphone. Tank commanders were getting ready to open fire, ordering high-explosive projectiles into each breech, deciding whether shells should be set on 'percussion' or 'delay'. I was about to switch to intercom and make our preparations when the regimental net came to life again.

'Orders. You will not close with objective. Halt well clear of perimeter. Make feint attack by maintaining fire into area until ordered to stop. Real attack will be made from other side by friends on left. Acknowledge. Over.'

I gave my call-sign and acknowledged, 'Wilco. Out.'

Now I had to catch Mac before A Squadron was in among the trees of the village. I did not even try 'B' set, switching instead to intercom.

'Albert, get me alongside the major's tank again, on the move.' As Albert changed down and the tank lurched to respond, I was writing the order in chinagraph on a sheet of notebook. 'Bill, take over the tank, no collisions! Keep Albert alongside and halt when the major halts.'

We were level. Headphones off. I was outside the turret on the sloping bin. Under one flying arm the map board caught the breeze as I thrust off with both boots. At first the board seemed to help with lift, then it turned my whole body slightly left. I landed awkwardly on Mac's thin running-board, stumbled, grasped the aerial base with my right hand, pulling up behind his turret, yelling and gesticulating down into it to halt.

As the driver applied the brakes, I could brace myself against the back of the turret and extract the paper message from between talc and map, thrusting it down at the operator, who held it unceremoniously under his deaf commander's nose.

Mac's reaction showed that he was still 'with it'. He pressed his microphone prestle switch and halted all troops at once, still with an interval between them and the village perimeter. Then he looked up at me and actually grinned. It was quite the warmest communication I was to experience from him, the only one I should remember. He must have been quite relieved not to have to drive the squadron in among the trees to meet whatever was there, and then to hang on to the gain without infantry support.

I looked at Mac's head. The bloody handkerchief was now held against the wound area by one headphone. Blood still seeped out below it, smudging down into his collar.

'Why don't you let Tony take over?'

Deaf or not, his reply was nearly as audible as the question: 'Get stuffed!'

I asked the operator what about putting a proper dressing on it.

'Won't have it, sir. Says it's only a scratch. He seems quite silly at times.'

I was given no chance to persist. Mac, having ordered his troops to pour fire into the fortified village, switched to intercom and ordered, 'Driver, advance.'

I leapt for my life back towards my own tank, skidding on a bin and crashing the map board against a cupola hatch lid. Mac was moving to a position from which he could join in the fire fight. I climbed back into turret and manoeuvred Albert so that we could do the same.

Tony, further left, had already opened up with his close-support 95 mm, while along the line the bell muzzles of the forward troops' 75 mms were recoiling as projectiles spurted on their way, then smoking blue until the next round followed. The sun shone brightly down on us all.

I reported to regiment, concluding that I expected to be off the air for a time, busy on intercom. The response was grudging: 'All right, but keep one good ear for when I order cease-fire. We must take care not to damage friends from the left.'

I acknowledged. With luck, we should hear 'A' set on induction through intercom, but I asked Bill to make a point of switching to 'A' set for a count of ten every time he had loaded the next shell. It was Bill's turn to grin. He knew he would have to give proper attention to keeping the 75 mm loaded from the bins, then tapping the gunner each time the breech closed, ready to fire.

My experience of commanding 75 mm gunfire was about ten minutes one misty morning on a range in Scotland, when my results (in the infantry I had been a rifle marksman) disgusted me. I knew now that Stanley was not too confident as a gunner, so I thought to do something to raise his morale and perhaps my own simultaneously.

The village revealed no obvious targets in gun emplacements, pillboxes or trenches, no doubt too well camouflaged. The farm buildings looked like farm buildings, solidly built and probably reinforced. One had a long, red-tiled roof. I remembered a remark someone made about tiled roofs at the Oxford tactical course.

'Put one on delay, Bill, and load. Seventy-five traverse left, 400, on!' The traverse stopped. 'Stanley, can you see that lovely red-tiled roof?' He assented. 'Just in case the OP controlling those stonks we've had is operating from there, I want you to get a bull's-eye. Take your time, fire when on.'

I had just seen Bill reach across to tap Stanley's arm as the breech slid closed. I fancied I heard Stanley murmur as he pressed his eye socket against the telescope rubber: 'Oh, aye!'

The tank rocked as the gun recoiled. The immediate noise entered my right ear with real pain. The ejected shell-case hit the back of the canvas chute, then fell to the turret floor with a sound that was to become familiar: 'Phong!'

We watched, open-mouthed like kids before a firework spreads its glitter, Albert through his open driving aperture, Harry and Stanley through their telescopes, Bill and I out of our hatches. The shell entered the centre of the tiled roof, exploding not on impact but immediately inside the building, lifting many tiles into the air on our side and the other, baring an enormous area of roof.

'Ah!'

'There you are, Stanley. How's that for your début?'

'What's that, Skipper?'

'That was a very impressive start! I hope you're pleased with yourself.'

Other people now thought the rest of the roof made a satisfying target – not that any OP was revealed there. Perhaps it was because the whole area was becoming a Hades of flame and smoke, tree splinters and other debris.

I had seen nothing human there, even from my very first view. Somehow I felt grateful for that, perhaps others did too, and yet it was illusory because the enemy *was* there, no doubt making the most of available cover. We continued firing into the smoke.

Harry had gun control of his hull machine-gun but my impression was that his use of it was economical. He must have had feelings about shooting up farmhouses.

With every round phonging out of the 75 mm, a pain started at my right ear and travelled down the neck into somewhere below the collar-bone, becoming almost unbearable. Suddenly I was aware of the adjutant's voice on a distant regimental net: '75 stop!'

I spoke in great relief, then switched to 'A' set. Sure enough, A Squadron was now to cease firing, watch for friends who would finish the job from another direction, be prepared for defenders escaping on our side.

Acknowledging the order and signing to Bill to watch out, I doffed headphones, hoisted out, jumped down, ran the few steps to Big Mac's tank and mounted, using the impetus of the run, one foot on a roadwheel hub, the other instep onto the rim of the running-board, grabbing something handy and hoisting up to the turret.

Mac had ceased firing too. I grabbed down at his shoulder. He and the operator looked up. I shouted the order. The operator wrote it down but Mac, expecting it, was already ordering troops to cease fire before he read it to confirm.

As I climbed back into my own tank, the next stonk straddled us. Guns and heavy mortars had the range of our position to a tee, but our orders were to stay put and watch. On the right, C Squadron reported engaging an enemy Mark IV tank and several anti-tank guns. A troop of B Squadron was being brought up to watch the regimental right, mainly west of the Caen–Falaise road.

The stonk stopped. I found myself wondering what had happened to yesterday afternoon's Panthers, to last night's Tigers. A similar thought must have struck Big Mac: he now moved two troops to watch our rear.

Smoke surrounding our tanks was slow to clear, but in Bras village the blurred scene was now exacerbated as Shermans invisible to us pumped more 75 mm shells into it from the other side, apparently half-left from our position. In time the gunfire eased, reducing to intermittent bursts of Browning machine-gun fire from Sherman hulls and turrets. Then through gaps in the smoke and flames we could see a company of the armoured brigade's motor battalion, operating in small groups, covering each other forward, fire and movement at the double, clearing ruins, dug-outs and other posts of surviving SS garrison.

Watching the riflemen do what I had trained to do until two years ago, I experienced momentary nostalgia and admiration. Knowing I was a more comprehensively trained infantry than a tank officer, I was also aware that my infantry competence had never been tested in action among the enemy's shells and bullets. Much as I could applaud the performance of the motor company now, I had no wish to return.

Some of the Shermans became visible, both among and beyond the riflemen. For what it was, Bras was in British hands at last.

Suddenly regimental net reported losing tanks to 88 mm gunfire on the right. I traversed our turret in the general direction, scanned the area up to a thousand yards distant through binoculars, along the rising ridge as well as down the slope of a re-entrant: nothing firing and nothing moving anywhere. Were the enemy shots coming from tanks located higher up the ridge in the heat haze? There were several patches of sunken or dead ground between our position and the haze-obscured distance.

I ordered a few rounds from our own gun, on percussion, spread about in the nearer sectors: perhaps a blast would flap a camouflage net, draw some retaliation ... Nothing. Another tank was reported hit, B or C Squadron's? I had seen nothing fire the shot. I fired two more rounds, still with no effect.

'We have a few smoke, Skipper.'

Bill might have come to the end of one bin of HE, seen some smoke projectiles there and thought we could use them before we traversed to get at another bin. Equally well he might have thought they could resolve our present problem. I thought of the tactical course dictum that smoke is a two-edged weapon. I hesitated. Then 'A' set reported another tank casualty.

'We'll try a couple, Bill. Keep your fingers crossed.'

I picked an area 900 yards further along the ridge on its eastern edge, judging it to intervene between the regiment and whatever gunsights might be trained on us from beyond. We put down the two smoke and a third which Bill produced. None of us had seen 75 mm smoke used before.

In what felt like still air under a sizzling sun, the initial effect looked negligible. As the little distant puffs developed, spreading and thickening, we could see that there was some kind of a local white screen. Then slowly, where we could have sworn there had been no wind, the screen began moving back towards us. Light airs from the south! Another tank was reported hit. I winced. The tactical course had been right: it would have been better if I had never used the stuff.

Next moment C Squadron announced spotting an 88 mm gun emplacement they had previously knocked out which had now sprung to life again. They silenced it once more, and our tank losses from armour-piercing shot ceased for the time being. The emplacement must have been in one of the patches of dead ground to us but visible to someone further right in C Squadron, and closer than where I had put down the smoke. I had begun to feel better about it when the thought occurred to me that the

88 mm crew might have taken advantage of that white cloud of my creation as it moved slowly north. How could we know? The cloud had disappeared now, leaving nothing but speculation.

I poured a mug of drinking-water for each. Harry said he was buttering biscuits and carving bully beef. Stanley asked if he could risk getting out for a leak. From the higher ground further south, enemy guns answered him by plastering us once more. I suggested Bill might extract an empty shell-case from the bottom of our gun's canvas chute and pass it to Stanley for the emergency. This took a minute or so. Stan said he would try. In the event he could not manage anything while seated on the gunner's stool. I flattened myself against the back of the turret so that he could stand almost upright and try again. The enemy stonk ceased, and with it Stanley announced his personal relief.

It proved catching. Harry asked if Stan could pass him the shell-case for use in the forward compartment. Stanley traversed the turret until Harry could reach through and take the case from him. Harry banged his face on the hull Besa stock as he levered himself up to the edge of his seat to use the improvised container.

Albert might as well use the thing while it was there. He knocked the case and spilled a drop in getting it past the gear lever located between his knees. By the time he had finished, Bill was ready to reach forward and take it. As another stonk began, he added his own contribution. Then he looked enquiringly across the gun breech at me. I took delivery cautiously just behind and below the gun. The long brass cylinder was heavier than I expected, and really warm.

I was just performing when on radio all squadron commanders were summoned to order group at a rendezvous given in letter code. Thoughtful always, Bill wrote it down for me. I finished what I had begun before grabbing the microphone to acknowledge the order. Fastening my thin metal fly-buttons, I pitched the no-longer-empty shell-case out of the cupola as clear of the tank as I was capable. I knew we were all hot, tired and apprehensive. The dispatch of the liquid-filled case triggered in me a brief euphoria. Switching to intercom, I announced that a valuable contribution had just been made to the local French agriculture. The engulfing stonk stopped as if on cue.

I directed Albert to drive us alongside Major Mac's tank. *En route* Harry was chuckling that what I had pitched out of the top was unlikely to do the Frogs much good. Then I stepped across to convey the summons. Mac traced the rendezvous reference on his map before looking up at me.

'Come on, then!'

The yeomanry had an order group drill, which older hands like Bill knew well. This was my first time. Squadron commanders took their rear links with them, leaving seconds-in-command in charge of the squadrons. So our tank moved off to accompany Mac at about a hundred yards interval, Tony and I exchanging mock American salutes as the squadron was left entirely to his command.

The selected RV was in the open, perhaps half-way up a long, wide slope. To my mind, without doubt it was substantially exposed to enemy view from higher up the main ridge. To be fair, there was probably nowhere within a mile of the regiment's present position that was not under enemy observation, unless it was back at Cormelles factory or its adjoining wood.

The Oxford course had taught that medium artillery in sufficient concentration could substantially damage tanks. In my judgement, as we approached the RV, it was only the extent to which our squadron had been dispersed that had kept down tank casualties from the repeated stonks.

The four tanks of RHQ were already positioned quite close together in the open. Tanks carrying Mac and the other two squadron commanders arrived from their respective locations and halted nearby, the majors dismounting with their map boards and climbing onto the back of the CO's Cromwell for the O-group. The escorting rear links halted clear of the main cluster, in my case about

150 yards uphill from it. I was careful to make sure my 'driving-mirror' fixed above the cupola was not reflecting towards the southern arc.

The seven tanks below appeared to have switched off engines. Albert asked if we should do the same. I reflected on probably the years of the regiment's training exercises in Britain (that I had missed) when this drill must have been practised in all kinds of places, so that it was now second nature to everyone except me. The only real difference then would have been that there was no real enemy to watch it.

'Keep the engine running, Albert.'

He set the hand throttle at something over a thousand revolutions, tightening the wing-nut on it, and I checked that the exhaust was putting out no smoke at all. Then we waited.

The conclave was left quite some time unmolested. The essential orders must have been effectively communicated when we saw a first major jump down, run to his own tank and mount. The engine started with the usual initial smoke cloud. Big Mac followed suit, reaching the side of his vehicle as a first ranging shot burst on the command group's downhill side. It was followed rapidly by a bracketing shot, landing between the order group and our tank. Big bursts, I reckoned, at least 150 mm or else heavy mortars. No sign where they were firing from.

'Ready to move, Albert!'

He reached to twist the wing nut, cut his revs, flicked a tiller bar. The gear moved cleanly into first as the whole tank wiggled.

In the group down the slope, Mac had disappeared into his turret. His engine started with another smoke puff. Another moment and he would be away.

When the enemy opened up, he must have concentrated his heaviest available weapons. The order group disappeared from view in an instant, but some of the bursts also landed uphill from the group, left and right of our tank, blasts that made themselves felt.

'Driver, advance, speed up, change up. Driver, left!'

Albert let in his clutch, accelerating. The 'Old Girl' hurtled as she had been pointing, towards somewhere left of where we had last seen RHQ, our speed down the slope enabling the left-turning circle in second or third gears at a pace not possible if we had had to pull away up the slope. I kept my head above cupola to zigzag Albert and avoid minor craters if they loomed through the impaired visibility, which was worse at his level than from turret top. I was not entirely successful at that speed and we tilted once or twice for a second before righting.

Suddenly we were clear of the shambles, climbing the slope diagonally under a hot sun, and I was sweating all over. Must locate Mac.

'Driver, halt. Bloody marvellous driving! Sorry I was a bit sharp back there, Albert.'

'I could tell you meant business, Skip. I reckon we're well out of that lot. I'm sweating like a pig!'

Harry spoke up: 'The earth was shaking. I 'ope no one caught a direct hit.'

Down the slope, several tanks had pulled outside the target area. I recognized Mac's from the white triangle on turret side. He halted, waiting to see what had happened at RHQ when the detonations should cease and the smoke thin out, which now seemed to happen as suddenly as it had all begun. Mac stayed only a short while after that before grinding up the slope back towards the squadron. We conformed.

The major pulled up alongside Tony's tank. Tony and I joined Mac around his turret. The commander stood up on his pedestal, brought his map board above turret top. The orders were so simple. What we had just done to Bras, A Squadron on its own would now do to Hubert Folie. Begin our move south of Bras at once. The same friends from the left would do the actual occupation of the Folie. A battalion from the infantry brigade was relieving the motor company in Bras. The rest of our regiment would stay put until the new infantry was firmly established.

Then Mac told us of the order-group experience: 'Tim's been killed, back of an HQ tank. Direct hit went through the engine covers.'

Tim Peck was the best-loved squadron commander. Tony had served long with him in C Squadron, I for a few months. Mac had been his second-in-command. Every soldier in C would grieve for his loss. I could see Big Mac trying to conceal how much he was affected.

'Come on then. We've got a job to do!'

Tony and I moved instantly. It was only as I settled back in my own turret that I recalled that Mac now had on a proper field dressing covering his wound; only later I heard it was the adjutant who had insisted, and the binding had been accomplished at the order group.

Hubert Folie was perhaps half a mile off. At times such a mix of gunfire baulked our approach along the ridge in a confusion of smoke, noise and cascades of earth that it was hard to see who was hit or what was happening. At other times everything went quiet and we edged further forward, not as one squadron now but using fire and movement by troops.

During one of the quieter intervals Tony persuaded Big Mac to let his crew drive him out to a rendezvous we arranged with the regimental medical officer, and Tony took command of the squadron. I was not near enough to say goodbye when Mac was driven off, and probably he wanted to avoid any goodbyes. In my mind I gave him full marks for pluck and for the squadron's achievement. To like him was still more than I could manage.

Light was beginning to fade by the time we had completed our task. The other regiment and the motor company were firmly into Hubert Folie. We stood by for counter-attack on stubble that was both scarred and scorched, the evening air above it blurred with drifting smoke from every kind of weapon and shellburst. Albert could switch off engine for a while.

I reported completion to regiment, swivelled the cupola mirror to see the immediate outside situation, then put my head out of the turret to make a more thorough inspection. That was when I noticed to the left rear of the tank a dozen soldiers in field grey, huddled together in a shallow pit. Intuitively my fingers reached across to the left side of my belt to flip open the press button of my infantry-type revolver holster, my right hand grasping the butt and withdrawing the Smith & Wesson. Even as I held the weapon, I realized that these were not men about to leap onto the tank. They were so still they must either be wounded or dead.

Then one or two of them were moving slowly. One was drawing a cape closer around his comrade. I switched to intercom, announced what I had seen, asked Harry to cover me while I got down to take a closer look. Harry swung back his hatch, clambering out onto the running-board with his pistol.

I was about to leave the turret when regiment called for supply requirements. I shouted to Harry to stay put while I answered on 'A' set: 'Wait. Out.'

Tony answered promptly on 'B' set. It was my decision, he said, now I was second-in-command. I pictured him grinning as he said it.

'I reckon one of each; might even need two of ammunition.'

'Be on the safe side; we've used a lot.'

I called regiment and it was done.

Then I got out. Harry reckoned there had not been much movement in the shallow pit. I approached them via the rear of the tank so as not to obscure Harry's view.

In the failing light – insufficient to read epaulettes for rank or arm of service – I saw that most of them were slumped against the shallow wall. They had perhaps been here for some time, waiting for the help that never came, but dressings were in place on wounds, and all had made the most of greatcoats and waterproofs for protective warmth and to reduce the effects of shock. Most faces looked ashen. There were personal weapons lying in the hollow, none close to the hand of its owner. Yes, they had been left too long. Some might already be dead.

I looked at the one with the wide-open eyes that were not glazed, the one who had been muttering at Harry.

'Wasser ... brauchen Wasser' – 'Water ... need water.'

There was an uncorked water-bottle on the ground. I picked it up. It had a jagged shrapnel hole in it. I substituted a discarded steel helmet, took it back up the tank to the turret top and spoke on intercom to the crew.

'These Jerries are in poor shape. Can we spare them some water?'

I knew we had little left, for it had been a thirsty day. Would the water cart reach us again tonight?

Albert spoke first: 'Poor bastards! It might be us tomorrow. Let's give 'em what we can.'

No one dissented. Bill wiped the inside of the helmet with a fistful of clean cotton-waste, then trickled in from the third jerrican, the only one where the tap still delivered without undoing the clamp and tipping the container forward. Half-way up the helmet were two small vent-holes, not visible in the dimness of the turret. Bill turned off when he felt the water spurting out of them, then warned me as he lifted the crude container up onto turret top. Inevitably I spilled some in getting down to ground-level; even resting the thing on the running-board it rocked as I jumped; but most of the content was intact.

I heard the radio guttering. Bill acknowledged, then called to me that squadron was to move, a map reference in code.

'Get Captain Venner on "B" set. Pass him the order and the reference as it stands if I'm not back when he answers.'

Bill began his call. I turned to make the few steps to the hollow, water slopping in the curved container. I put the helmet carefully into the usable hand of the spokesman, sensing his revulsion at the idea of drinking water in a steel helmet, or was it my own? Then, not drinking from it himself, with so much effort he moved onto his knees, spilling a little more, then rousing a first comrade to drink.

I returned to the tank as Bill finished speaking. Tony acknowledged. Engines started up. I groped for a screened light to decode. The spot was back down the hill. The squadron moved, Albert following Tony's tank. I radio'd regiment, referring to the map co-ordinates I had given for the place we were just leaving, asking if the MO could do something for the dozen wounded enemy.

'He has many calls at present. I will pass your message, but no promises. Out.'

It had been an elastic day, stretching time and nerves. I did not know it then, but from its usual sixty-one, the regiment was down to twenty-three tanks.

7 All Change

Bill and I had been awake since more than two hours before dawn. We should therefore take again the final turn on guard so as to sleep at the earliest opportunity. None of us could sleep until the supply echelon arrived, and there would be much to unload. Tony ran the squadron differently from Big Mac, and in the open laager HQ was located more centrally than on the previous night. When the lorries arrived at the head of the column, it seemed quite a way to walk with stores to the rear-link tank. The night was darker than its predecessor, due to cloud.

I carried a first couple of 4½ gallon petrol jerricans down the line to the waiting Albert and returned for more. It might have been on my second or third run that I woke to find myself sitting on one can, my right hand firmly grasping the smooth handle of the other, my beret-covered head butted into the upper half of some tank's middle road-wheel. Had I been there two minutes or twenty? I pushed guiltily to my feet, conscious at last of my extreme tiredness, lumbered with the two cans rearwards. Other figures passed me in the dark, going back empty-handed for more stores. Albert received the cans as if there had been no delay. No one was speaking; night silence was observed, aided by great fatigue.

I went back for an assortment of 75 mm ammunition, cradling it over two weak arms, hoping I should not fall asleep in its possession. In the rear link, Bill was hand-traversing the turret to remove lids one by one and refill the ammo bins. Harry and Stan had just unloaded on him. He passed me down an empty drinking-water jerrican.

At the head of the column, Tony was propped on a tank's front apron, both feet on the ground, perhaps dozing, one eye watching the emptying of lorries. Even in the dark I sensed the slight smile on his normally rather serious face. He had commanded a squadron for over four hours, during which time no more tanks or crews had been lost. He would dismiss the echelon when the drop was complete. I could fill my silver can at the water cart and turn in.

20 July did not begin too auspiciously for me. The next thing was when Stanley tried to rouse me for the final turret watch. An hour later, when I at last stirred, he told me he had given up trying, because I had made no response at all. He had simply extended his own spell. It was something I have not experienced before or since, and I hope it increased my powers of understanding and tolerance. For now, I thanked Stanley in great humility, apologizing that he would have little sleeping-time before stand-to. Bill whispered that they had had job enough to wake *him*. He was not quite sure he *was* awake.

Together we waited for the dawn, speculating whether we should again be an early target for 88 mm twilight sights, musing whether help had reached the group of enemy wounded, wondering if we should lead a renewal of the divisional assault in the morning, not enthusing at the prospect.

In the event, nothing fired at us throughout stand-to, nor during a breakfast hour beyond that. After a long time without orders or news, we learned that the division was recalled into corps reserve. During another hot day but with more cloud build-up, the regiment moved back to the outskirts of Demouville, where some medium artillery, across the River Orne at last, were digging in their 5.5s beside us.

When the rain began, I was not the only one who threw back his head to feel the great drops smack down upon dry lips in a tired face. What followed was a daylight thunderstorm that turned most of the corridor into a quagmire in which wheeled vehicles began to bog. The weather, like our attack, had broken.

While the regiment relaxed at last on the 20th, the bomb-plot to assassinate Hitler was being played out in East Prussia. We really had no idea what was going on amongst our enemy, only that his western armies were putting up a toll-taking defence.

On the day before our big attack, the 17th, Rommel had been returning to his HQ from a tour of the ten-or-more-mile-deep defences that would blunt and then block the apparent British design, when his car was individually assailed by a roving RAF fighter plane. It crashed, killing the driver, Rommel himself being critically injured and removed to hospital.

Instead of replacing Rommel, von Kluge, who had succeeded von Rundstedt as commander in the west, took on Rommel's command of Army Group B as well. Now, on the 20th, von Kluge received at least two phone calls from the bomb-plotters telling him Hitler was dead and seeming to expect some significant action from him. 'Clever Hans' is said to have hung up without answering on both occasions, and to have done nothing.

Later in the day, when German forces learned of their Führer's survival, senior commanders like von Kluge could picture the process by which the Gestapo would be beginning to identify anyone connected with the plot. The performances of the 7th Army and the newly designated 5th Panzer Army in Normandy gave no sign to us, the adversaries, of being in any way impaired by the impending Gestapo process, which generals and others could expect would offer good cover for paying off old scores not necessarily related to the plot.

Seconds-in-command were sent off to reconnoitre harbour areas for the regiment west of Caen. I took leave of my crew, hoping to see them again inside twenty-four hours, and was carried off in the squadron scoutcar recently brought forward into the mud. Back we went over the river and canal bridges and round by the north of the ruined city to some unspoiled fields in which the squadrons, RHQ and the echelon could be well spread out.

I had made the harbour reconnaissance for A Squadron, but once RHQ moved into the adjoining large field, a further general post of the more senior officers took place as it had after the June action. Oblivious that in a pitched battle in southern France the SS were annihilating the lightly armed Maquis, our yeomanry unit proceeded with another reorganization.

'Sandy' Saunders, senior captain from HQ Squadron, took command of A, with Tony remaining as his second-in-command. I was posted as second-in-command to C Squadron, whose 2 I/C during the recent action, John Finnis, became squadron commander, with Alastair Hetherington moving from regimental intelligence officer to be rear link.

Bill, Albert, Harry and Stan formed up to the new major of A, asking to be transferred with me to C. I said when asked that I should be delighted for them to move across with me. There was a conference between two new squadron majors and the adjutant, concluding that it would not be done. Arrived at C, I took over a tank with a 95 mm close-support gun and a different crew. The old foursome, who had spent the war in A – but what a changed A it was now! – exchanged good wishes with me for the survival of us all, and I left.

I had known John Finnis when he was second captain in C, a fairly genial but far from close relationship. I suspected that what we had in common was a prizing of our personal privacy. He, Alastair and I now discussed division of areas of responsibility both out of action and in. My impression was that John would make a commander I could happily work with, and the three of us a good team.

Here, on good green grass away from the sound of gunfire, the regiment could catch up on its sleep, with only nocturnal mosquitoes to disturb it by invading newly washed hair. The squadron got on with some initial bathing as the weather recovered and sun warmed the water. I went into division to draw pay for those requiring it, also visiting the dentist for a repair. I was able to write longer letters to my beloved and to my parents, but not to mention the recent action until a fortnight had elapsed. Besides the routine function of censoring, there were informal letters to write to bereaved families.

B echelon arrived with our heavier personal kit in waterproofed ammunition boxes. This got me a much-needed fresh change of underwear and a look in a real mirror, as distinct from the small metal one I carried in my inside battledress pocket. I was amazed at the sight of my sheer weatherbeaten scruffiness, which persuaded me to perform an extra shave and then seek out in the echelon a soldier who made a spare-time occupation of cutting hair. Some folding chairs and a small tent appeared for the setting-up of a very temporary C Squadron mess.

A letter came from the late Major Peck's sister – Tim had not been married apparently – requesting that his kit be divided among his comrades.

'That's Keith's job, administration.'

John tried to sound nonchalant, but he had known Tim too long and too well to face the task himself. Tim's ammunition box was brought. I removed the waterproofing and got on with the job. It gave me time to reflect that, during my short time last year in C Squadron, I had only had cause to think well of Tim, who had cared about everyone in the squadron. He, who would surely have made an adored father to a family of any size, had not even embarked on one. With all the comradeship we achieved as temporary soldiers, how very little most of us knew, or enquired, about each others' lives, commitments or dreams outside the service existence.

No official information came about the regiment's or the division's losses just sustained, nor one word about those of the infantry formations on the flanks of the corridor, and of the tank units that supported them. Infantry division casualties had in fact been far steeper than those of the armoured formations in the corridor, and the overall

British tank losses in the operation have been put at over 400.

Our replacement tanks now came, with their guns solid in grease, taking hours of work to remove. I was reminded of a Liverpool-Irish soldier in Britain whose practice for dealing with gun grease was to boil petrol over an open fire, then pour it into the barrel at maximum elevation. For this he had been removed from tank crews to become the C of E padre's driver in the celestial half-track.

The training and experience records of crew reinforcements bore enquiry to achieve their most appropriate absorption, which had a bearing on their own but also on the whole squadron's morale. Fortunately John Finnis and the SSM knew their original squadron very well. It was also an active time for my newly acquired administrative role, apart from the odd replacement radio to see installed, while tank maintenance itself gave few headaches because the Cromwell – engine, transmission, tracks and traverse – was such a reliable vehicle. I picked up a few tips about the 95 mm gun from Tony Venner, finding that my new gunner had not fired one before, so we started level.

Alastair came back from visiting friends at Divisional HQ with the suggestion that we might make up a modest dinner party to eat at a French establishment recommended by Charles Pidduck, the general's ADC. John said he would hold the squadron fort, so I drove the jeep with Alastair navigating, Tony from A Squadron and Jimmy Grimstone, our own senior troop leader. We picked up Charles at Div. *en route*.

The country meal in the open air was juicy rump steak with new potatoes, accompanied by a glass or two of a Barsac the withdrawing Wehrmacht had overlooked. It all cost the equivalent in francs of about 13 shillings a head – one day's pay for a subaltern, not much less than a captain's.

With daylight still left, at Charles's suggestion we drove to some cliffs overlooking the Channel coast. A cool, stiffening breeze off the sea dimmed the last rays of a red sun soon swallowed by clouds. Every kind of craft rode out the restlessness of the water for as far as our vision reached. Perhaps we all thought of England, invisible to the north. It was Tony, with a French wife somewhere on the north side of that broad expanse of sea, who broke our silence:

'This is where we came in.'

Next afternoon work at C Squadron was easing off except for a small working party priming grenades in a hollow clear of the lines of tanks. John sat on a folding chair with his sleeves rolled up, breathing audible satisfaction at having just personally sewn the crowns of new rank onto the epaulettes of his battledress.

He picked up a short-barrelled Luger pistol newly acquired from Tony, who had found it near Hubert Folie and now wanted to get rid of it. Lodged in a corner of his turret with the safety catch on, the thing had fired at least one shot 'all on its own' as the tank lurched over uneven ground. Someone might have got hurt. Tony warned that it must have a hair trigger. John said he would manage it.

I watched him withdraw the magazine from inside the pistol-grip before I turned away to relax at the trestle table and sip a mug of tea.

'I expect the safety catch is just loose,' he was saying.

At the same table, Alastair bit into a slice of freshly buttered bread smothered in tinned marmalade. He looked past me across the field towards a distant RHQ, then tensed up, staring hard through his metal-rimmed spectacles.

'Somebody tell me I'm not seeing things!'

It was a hot enough day for mirages. I looked in the same direction. We both stood up.

A tall, ungainly figure moved unhurriedly towards us, the beret bulging with clean white bandaging. The face wore what might have been a self-conscious grin. John looked up and saw him.

'Good God! Macgillicuddy!' Loudly he called to a mess staff trooper: 'More tea, please, for Major Mac!'

I walked to the mess lorry for another folding chair. As I

returned, Alastair was listening to Big Mac saying he had decided in the UK that the doctors were wrong about his head being bad enough to take a holiday. Walking out of hospital, he had had no difficulty in getting lifts back to the unit. The colonel said he was to take over C Squadron.

As we waited to learn more, a pistol report redirected our attention. John still sat in his chair as if bemused, regarding the jinxed Luger in one hand, and the blood flowing from the other.

'What happened, John?' Big Mac commanded the squadron already.

A trooper put down Mac's tea and struggled to force his field dressing out of its tight-sewn battledress pocket.

'How did it happen, John?' We were all aware of Mac's persistence.

Before we could hear any more, there was a stampede of feet from the grenade hollow. The corporal called out: 'This way, man! Move! Don't just sit there!'

There was a pause before the head and shoulders of the last member of the priming party appeared over the lip of the hollow, moving as if in a dream. The grenade detonated at that moment. The dreamer moved perhaps another half-pace, then sank face downward in the grass. When I got to him, he was whimpering quietly, a distinct whistle as he breathed. Someone pulled up his shirt. There was a quarter-inch puncture in the back, above the waist but near the spine. Purple, it scarcely bled, outside.

'Double across for the MO, ambulance!'

Someone departed, running, as Jimmy Grimstone joined us. He knew the wounded trooper. We looked our concern at each other. The corporal in charge of the priming operation began to explain what had happened.

'I'd just been saying, "There's Major Mac come back to us." I heard this click, and the lad was just sitting there, looking at the grenade he was holding in his hand. He'd pulled out the pin, and the lever was still in the air. Four seconds!

'I knocked the thing out of his hand and lugged him to his feet – or almost – as we all ran out of the dell for cover.

He started off in one direction, then he must have turned back to follow me when I shouted, and it caught him.

'I could have thrown it, sir, but there wasn't anywhere safe to throw it.'

I nodded.

The wounded youngster was restless, breathing fast, sweat standing out on him, moaning quietly in pain. He seemed past speech but still conscious. One blanket was folded under his head, another we tucked round him. The restlessness continued. No sound of the ambulance. On a thought, I put my hand into an inside battledress pocket and pulled out a small tube issued to me weeks ago in case of need. I showed it to Jimmy Grim'.

'What do you think, Jimmy?'

'Don't know much about morphia. I've still got my ampoule somewhere in my kit, unused ... He certainly looks distressed.'

'I think I'd better,' I said. 'My decision God help me, I hope I'm right.'

Removing the cap, I plunged the tiny needle into a buttock through the trousers, held it in close and squeezed the tube empty. Then we wrote on the victim's forehead in chinagraph what he had had administered and when, just as we remembered it from a first aid film. When the ambulance arrived, his condition seemed no different. John Finnis went too, his left hand a bundle of dressing.

At dinner Big Mac asked who had given the trooper morphine. I acknowledged.

'You've probably killed him!' Mac turned to Alastair. 'Don't you reckon so?'

Alastair looked straight at our new commander.

'I see no reason for saying that, Major, unless the lad was going to die anyway. Keith made his decision in good faith, and he'll worry about it more than you will.'

'That's enough!' Big Mac glowered at us both. His whole attitude seemed to bode ill for our next action.

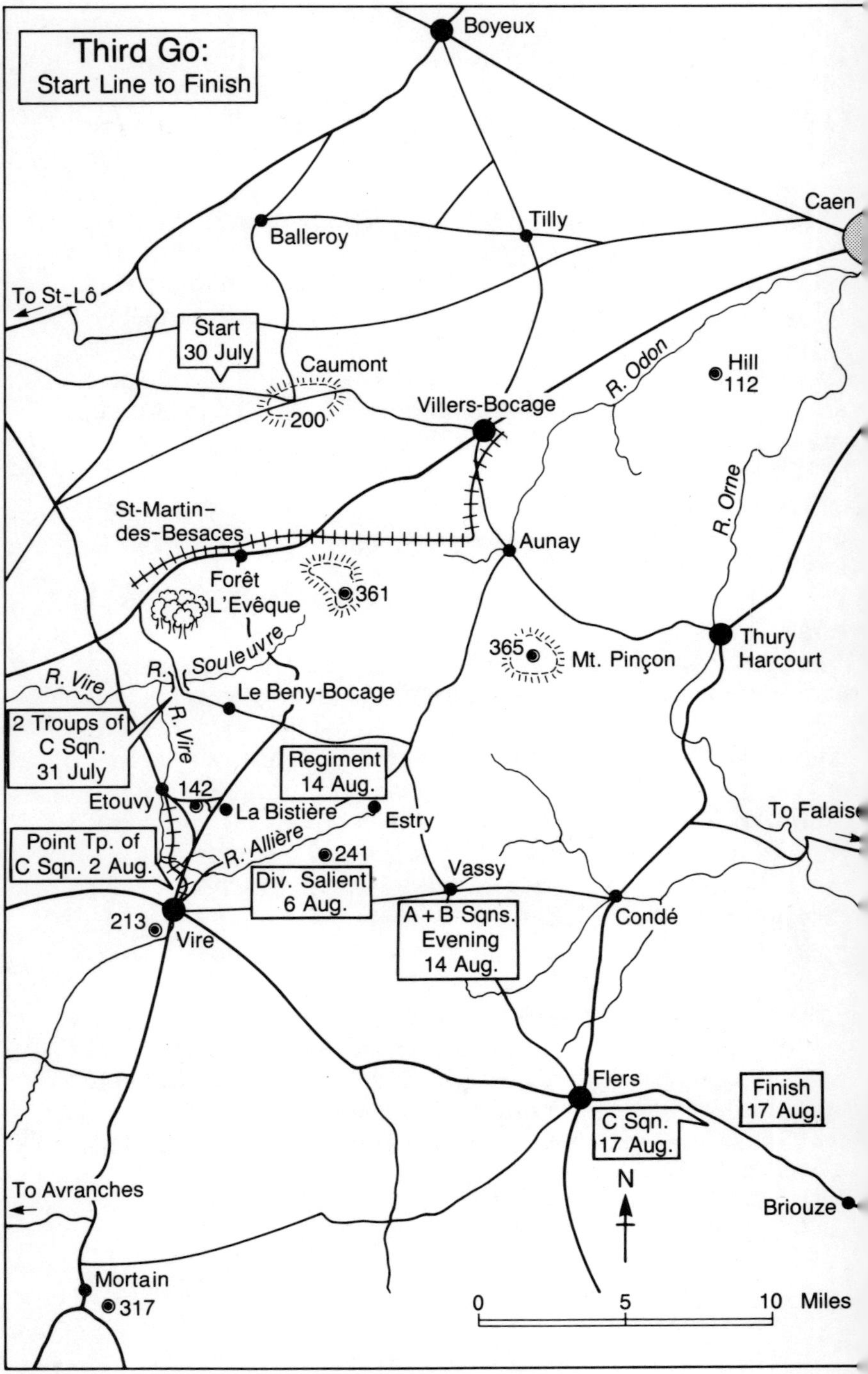
Third Go:
Start Line to Finish
Boyeux
Caen
Balleroy
Tilly
To St-Lô
Start
30 July
Caumont
200
Villers-Bocage
R. Odon
Hill
112
R. Orne
St-Martin-
des-Besaces
Aunay
Forêt
L'Evêque
361
365
Mt. Pinçon
Thury
Harcourt
R. Vire
R.
Souleuvre
Le Beny-Bocage
2 Troups of
C Sqn.
31 July
R. Vire
Regiment
14 Aug.
Etouvy
142
La Bistière
Estry
To Falaise
Point Tp. of
C Sqn. 2 Aug.
R. Allière
241
Vassy
Div. Salient
6 Aug.
213
Vire
A + B Sqns.
Evening
14 Aug.
Condé
Flers
Finish
17 Aug.
C Sqn.
17 Aug.
N
To Avranches
Briouze
Mortain
317
0
5
10
Miles

8 In the Lead

The Americans assaulted Panzer Lehr's positions west of St-Lô on 25 July, in the wake of a moon-cratering preliminary by 1,500 Fortresses and with the support of over 500 guns. They advanced two miles.

That was the day a Canadian attack on the Bourgebus ridge – from which we had so recently been withdrawn – was bloodily repulsed. The Desert Rats' armoured brigade had remained in the area to support the Canadians until nearer the end of the month as their own armoured division began to arrive. The Canadian attack was effective in preventing the 5th Panzer Army from releasing armour to the 7th Army as it reeled from the American onslaught.

On the 26th US progress continued, finding the enemy had few reserves and little depth where the strike had been made, so the first of the American armour exploited the gap to drive on Marigny and Canisy, the eastern column finding sufficient lack of opposition that its tanks pressed on by night.

On the 27th the western American column made for Coutances, but pressure on their flank by the 2nd Panzer Division prevented entry to the town that day. On the 28th two new US armoured divisions joined the advance. By nightfall the American line was fifteen miles beyond its starting-points on the 25th. The information reaching us in our grassy respite place was that it looked as if the Americans were getting somewhere at last.

Montgomery, as overall land commander, was quick to exploit the US VII Corps' success by directing British armour to push southwards on the immediate left of American XIX Corps, which was attacking from ground held to the east of the break-out and had not yet itself advanced above a mile or so. Our division (the 11th) would be on the British right, but first it had to get to its start-line near Caumont from its present location just west of Caen.

On 28 July I was despatched in C Squadron scoutcar to select and prepare a tank harbour within a four-figure map reference that was in among our United States allies. British 7th Armoured had passed near to and east of American-held Caumont on their first penetration to Villers-Bocage in June, but the map square towards which the scoutcar now had to take me was further west than any British unit had yet been.

Nothing is ever simple: if it were not enough that our mission had to thrust, check and cajole its way across every intervening formation's north–south centre-line, with their unending supply and reinforcement columns, the scoutcar was obliged to take an additional passenger. A lance-corporal had developed symptoms of an acute appendicitis. As our own divisional arrangements were becoming fluid, my task was now to stop at an intermediate rendezvous along our route, there to wait for a particular medical vehicle which was collecting non-wounded casualties/people reporting sick, and conveying them to facilities nearer the beaches.

The Humber scoutcar was not the best conveyance for someone with pains in the gut. There was no way the patient could relax. Even stretched out on the engine cover he was at risk of toppling overboard unless he braced himself and hung on.

At several crossings of centre-lines I could get us through other people's columns only by mounting bumpy verges or diverting across country where the going looked feasible. The driver performed well and I contrived to attend to my map as well as shouting at column leaders and the occasional motor-cyclist traffic-controller, but at every fresh hazard our lance-corporal looked more poorly.

Eventually we reached the RV, parked on some grass clear of the moaning vehicle columns, and he could rest.

We waited two hours for the ambulance. Our charge was convinced his appendix would burst before he could be got into hospital. I talked to him about a sergeant I had known in the West Kents who had waited all day and most of one night in a similar condition and still been operated on in time. I spun out my tale but the patient was not to be reassured. The driver and I were relieved when the medical vehicle at last reported to take charge of him. We wished him well and closed the doors. The ungainly crate took its red crosses back into the main stream of northbound traffic and lumbered away. We were free, late, to press on towards our well-breeched allies.

A change in the nature of the country made itself felt. More up hill and down dale. More tree cover, complete woody enclosure for stretches. Narrower, twisting roads among fields surrounded by impenetrable hedges that grew out of a mud and stone wall tough as the castles of William the Norman. We were into the *bocage,* dense woodland. This was the country our allies had been fighting in.

The Americans in this part of XIX Corps sector had found one or two adjoining areas providing uninterrupted space enough to accommodate vast quantities of vehicles and stores under cover from aerial view. In recent hours they had contrived – with the Limeys' imminent arrival in mind – to vacate certain parts of the whole, at which one of their majors waved airily, inviting me to help myself. Our reception was casual but they clearly had plenty to get on with. I picked a squadron harbour with ready access to road. We parked the scoutcar.

I reported our choice to the US major, so he would not think there was a counter-attack if our Cromwells came in after dark, gratefully accepted his cup of coffee and declined with thanks the divided metal platter on which I recognized only chunks of undercooked swede, saying we had already begun heating the rations we had brought with us.

Most of the regiment moved only in the small hours of the 29th, so we had quite a long wait before Big Mac reached us and C Squadron settled down for one night in this undistinguished spot well south of Balleroy.

Next morning the regiment was part of the infantry brigade group, composed of two battalions, a Sherman unit and ourselves for the 0900 hours move off. C Squadron was in regimental reserve, which meant that our progress along the winding byroads past the west side of Caumont was full of stop and start. We carried a company of Herefords on our backs part of the way but at one of the halts they dismounted, having been called forward. Under the trees, as in the harbour area, we were screened from the 30 July weather, which began cloudy. Later on, some of the large open fields in arable or for pasture were seen to be soaking up the summer sun.

We could hear mortar and machine-gun fire in front of us from time to time. Combined with the delays, it told of the enemy resistance. We knew our brigade group was on the right of the division. I was watching curiously for signs of the US 5th Infantry Division, then the nearest formation of the American 1st Army.

Squadron HQ pulled onto a roadside clearing for a late lunch. Engines were switched off. Parallel with our line of advance to our right was a large open field, much longer than it was wide. After our halt had lasted perhaps a couple of hours or more, it was in this field that we first noticed our allies, the long files of their infantry making their way down both edges, and some in the centre, all going in the same direction as we had been until we stopped.

Looking at them over the hedge where road impinged on field, our crews waved in silent greeting, and some of the Americans waved back. They were evidently the leading elements of their outfit and expected to advance as if they might bump trouble at any time. More and more entered the field from way back, carrying their weapons, ammunition and kit. Eventually, reaching the forward end of the field, the point sections disappeared into the wooded area beyond and were gone from sight. Plenty more were coming behind, all steel-helmeted by order, in contrast to our crews wearing their comfortable berets. It was our first sight of an American fighting formation, and the impression was to persist and recur reinforced: what very large numbers – there were always more and more to come!

Alastair and Big Mac were beside the former's tank. Alastair had his headphones on. I imagined he would be reporting the sighting of our friends to RHQ. When an American colonel and his entourage strode out of the trees and made a bee-line for the squadron HQ tanks, I went to meet them just clear of where we were halted. The party had paused after breaking cover while a runner crashed up to the colonel, saluted and handed him a written message. I wondered if the performance might have been laid on for our benefit, but I saluted the colonel myself. He acknowledged and then shook hands.

I confirmed we were part of the British right and were in reserve, had not moved for two hours, that we could hear firing in front but knew no details. If I secretly hoped Mac would come over and say what he had learned, if anything, on Alastair's regimental net, I was disappointed, for as soon as he saw me talking to an American, he looked the other way as if listening to the radio, which perhaps he was.

The colonel acknowledged my information before excusing himself to use his walkie-talkie, a sizeable rectangular box with telescopic aerial which he pulled to its full length before speaking. He gave a call-sign, then stated his map position in clear, repeating it as if anyone listening was bound not to get it first time.

'No contact so far, except with friends. I am closing my battalion HQ on this point.'

I winced. To give an 'own troops' position in clear was a cardinal sin in British radio discipline. It crossed my mind whether perhaps our allies reckoned their walkie-talkies had such limited range that their procedure was secure anyway. The possibility left me unconvinced.

The arrival of another runner with a message gave me a chance to excuse myself and return to squadron HQ, which started up and moved on down the road. It was the last the squadron was to see of allies on the British right flank for several days.

If our own progress on that first day, 30 July, had been disappointing, and that of the 1st US Army on our right more so, the break-out forces further west – now in their sixth day – were really pouring through the breech, the US 4th Armoured Division by dusk reaching the key town of Avranches. Coincidentally the forces concerned were officially redesignated 3rd Army, which became operational that same day under George Patton. Brittany lay ahead of them, virtually undefended. More important, once clear of the *bocage* and the main weight of German Army Group B, the Americans could swing east to Le Mans and Alençon (just as Montgomery had directed Bradley in a document dated late June) on the way to encircling the enemy or driving for Paris, or both.

Meanwhile the bulk of Army Group B was still right in front of us, the British and Canadians reaching beyond Caen, and also of the Americans on our immediate right. At this stage and for some time yet, probably no one part of the enemy force – except its commander, 'Clever Hans' von Kluge, who was also supreme commander in the west – realized the army group's imminent peril of encirclement and annihilation.

The British armoured thrust from Caen had begun to convince the enemy high command that a second invasion was becoming less likely, whereon intact infantry formations began to be released from the 15th Army defending the Pas de Calais and Somme to make their way to Normandy at last. As these arrived and took over positions opposite the Canadians south of Caen, some of the Panzer elements previously committed in the front line could be disengaged and moved westward with the intention of countering the break-out. To reach that area they would need to cross the very line down which we had just begun advancing. We learned nothing of this in C Squadron, but in any case the process was in its very early stages as we harboured for the night of the 30th.

At the time of harbouring, our information was that the infantry brigade group ahead of us had encountered stiff resistance most of the day and taken casualties. One of our sister squadrons had lost two tanks on mines in a sunken road. The left-hand brigade group had also had mines to clear and had made slow progress, but its motor battalion intended pressing on methodically all night, hoping by dawn to reach the road to Caumont where it led out of St-Martin-des-Besaces.

A battalion of our infantry brigade group had in parallel the task of penetrating the lines of enemy with whom they had still been in contact at last light, with the object if possible of cutting the same road – the Caen – Avranches main – on the west side of St-Martin. A track through the thickly wooded country was found which appeared to be undefended. The smallest enemy detachment could have effected an ambush to disrupt their operation but the men of Shropshire took their chance. Single file, they moved cautiously through the darker-than-usual night until by dawn they straddled the main road.

At an early hour of daylight on the 31st, C Squadron was summoned to join the battalion just north of the road and help them secure their positions. We found a way down that proved to be clear of mines. The first task on arrival was to probe a short way to the west, giving some of the battalion an initial piggy-back. When they disembarked and deployed, Big Mac directed a couple of troops to cross road and railway line and reach the south side.

That was when some enemy guns, probably self-propelled, opened fire from further west, apparently straight down the railway line. A tank was hit.

The two troops got across the rails and looked for fire positions. When squadron HQ moved up to some bushes near the tank casualty, I got out and went over to it. A section of Shropshires moved past me tactically before I could reach the hull, but they were watching the next shrub cover.

Through the driver's aperture it looked as if downstairs had baled out. At least the tank had not caught fire. I mounted to the turret. A quick-firing enemy machine-gun loosed a short burst that seemed to pass close. On impulse I dropped down through the commander's cupola, stepping rapidly from pedestal to turret floor before breathing in a stench that provoked such a diaphragm reflex that I nearly took off outside again.

Closing my mouth tightly, I stared. The commander was gone or I should not have been able to descend. In front of me was the gunner, a hand still on the elevating wheel, head rolled aside from the rubber eyepiece of the telescope to jam against the inside turret wall, the eyes wide open and glazed like those of fish on the slab. No sign of breathing; he could hardly be alive. Round the other side of the gun, the operator's body was wedged almost upright between gun and turret wall. Where was his head? Then I could see the top of his spine jutting from the collar. The smell was explained too. The head was distributed in small deposits adhering to the inside of the turret wall, seemingly all the way round, with tufts of hair still growing out of some pieces. Who were they, these two? I could neither recognize them nor recall who had crewed this tank.

I made my exit from turret to engine covers as rapidly as possible, jumping down to ground-level at once, but no machine-gun fired this time, probably a tribute to the Shropshires' progress.

I was about to go back to my own tank when I saw a half-track approaching in the wake of the squadron. It stopped beside me, and a field ambulance MO got out. He was wearing a greatcoat, which struck me as odd, although the day was dull and had not warmed up. He was dark, with black eyes. For some reason I imagined him centuries earlier as a Pict raiding across Hadrian's Wall. The eyes were fixed on me now. Perhaps he had seen me descend from the tank. I think I was still a bit dazed.

'What's the score?' He nodded at the tank. Sure enough, his accent was Scots.

'An 88 hit, or something. Two chaps in there ...'

He was clambering up the tank, clumsily in his long topcoat. I called to him to mind the machine-gun covering the turret but he seemed not to heed. Grasping one hatch to steady himself, he glanced inside, then vaulted back down in front of me. He thrust both hands into his deep greatcoat pockets and addressed me in a kindly voice that also attempted to be matter-of-fact.

'They're dead. The human frame will put up with so much and no more. I expect you knew them.'

I could not answer. We nodded and returned to our vehicles, he being driven towards where the infantry had gone. There is more often something a doctor can do with at least some infantry casualties. It was decent of him to have stopped off at our tank.

I asked my operator what I had missed on squadron net. He said squadron commander seemed to be talking to the two troops that had crossed the railway further and further away from our present location. He could not understand why the rest of the squadron was not following them up.

An hour or so later squadron HQ also crossed the railway. Nothing fired at us. In the fringe of some tree cover we faced south and waited, engines off. Big Mac spoke occasionally with Alastair about a rear-link message. He explained nothing beyond: 'We're staying here.' I concluded that the rump of the squadron was remaining to secure the south-west of St-Martin. The three troops occasionally spotted enemy movement to the south. Sometimes they fired at it without much coming back at us.

There was little communication from the two troops that had gone off. I could understand their desire not to draw attention to themselves even on the ether, because they were getting deeper and deeper into enemy territory.

What had happened during the morning was that an armoured car patrol had found an undefended track through the Forêt l'Evêque. Coasting quietly through it and continuing a mile or two beyond the far end, the car crews came upon an undefended and intact bridge that carried the main St-Lô–Le Beny Bocage road over the River Souleuvre close to where it joins the River Vire. The patrol straddled the bridge and radio'd division for support.

Division had called our regiment, and while I was looking inside a stricken tank, Big Mac began talking the two troops into the same track through the forest, and on and on until they joined the Household Cavalry patrol some two hours after its arrival there. The small combined force was sitting round a key bridge ostensibly some four miles or more behind or into enemy lines, and no one was counter-attacking them yet. This was still all we knew at SHQ when the rations arrived before dusk, early because regiment thought we might be on the move later.

Separated from that force by some miles, I thought how creepy the silence must be around that bridge, wondering when a squad of Tigers might appear from among the trees to take them on. Undoubtedly enemy armour was being released from the east end of the Allied beachhead to move west against the break-out. We did not know it, but the 21st Panzer Division was at that moment driving hard for the Beny Bocage area. Keith Dyson, subaltern commanding one of the troops, and Sergeant Taylor with the other, would remember their participation in this bridge event that proved so significant.

Through the afternoon all that the bridge force saw – and shot up – were a few enemy vehicles bowling all unaware along the main road to the bridge: a lorry, a staff car, a motor-cyclist. More significantly, a prisoner was taken belonging to the 21st Panzer Division, together with his wireless code lists.

How had the enemy allowed such a penetration? Apparently the track had been a disputed responsibility on the boundary between the German 326th Infantry and 3rd Parachute Divisions. Our two troops that reached the bridge had first run the gauntlet of the guns firing down the railway, then bumped into and fired at some local enemy on the far side of the forest near La Ferrière. It seemed that the two enemy divisions remained unaware that their bridge had been captured, or perhaps each maintained that that action was the pigeon of the other. Certainly both were being slow to dispatch units to dispossess our small force.

Meanwhile the task of probing west along the railway line and the main Caen–Avranches road that ran roughly parallel with it was passed to B Squadron, who lost their leading tank to an anti-tank gun. They were able to shoot up a variety of enemy vehicles which drove along the road quite unaware that the British had blocked it at St-Martin. Later B was recalled to join the rest of the regiment south of St-Martin and watching south across a stream, while the recce troop overlooked the road leading south from there. In retrospect, I reckon division kept us there with the two battalions of infantry as a long-stop against the 21st Panzer drive.

When I had distributed rations to the main squadron and before it was getting dark, I proposed to Mac that I should take some for the two forward troops, using the squadron scoutcar now up with us, and push through the same forest track as the troops had used.

Mac's reply surprised me: 'You'll do no such thing. I need my second-in-command here.' He added that the two troops would not hurt without supplies for one night.

In the event I ought to have been grateful, because it transpired that the enemy had meanwhile closed the track through the Forêt l'Evêque. Alastair then heard on regimental net that other moves were in train.

If the Germans had not reacted locally to the bridge seizure, the British globally had. The 2nd Army switched its main strike to the extreme right, 11th Armoured, us. Division ordered its armoured brigade across the bridge. The leading Sherman regiment carrying infantry reached the small force holding it well before dark and perhaps about the time our squadron supply wagons had arrived.

Crossing the bridge, they found a battle group of 21st Panzer in the woods beyond, just forming up to attack. Engaged at once by the British spearhead, the enemy withdrew to fight another day.

Next day, 1 August, the armoured brigade entered Le Beny Bocage and went on to secure the high ground nearby. 21st Panzer kept clear of the division all day, whereas on our left and east of St-Martin, Guards Armoured were treated to a substantial counter-attack. On our right the Americans encountered such resistance that they remained well back. It appeared they were held by the intact right shoulder of the German 7th Army, the Guards by the left of the newly designated 5th Panzer Army, while our 11th Armoured was into a narrow gap between the two.

Our squadron moved late on that first day of August, crossed the river in the wake of the infantry brigade, and with it turned south, leaving Beny Bocage to the north-east. Its two troops rejoined, the squadron harboured early and rested up, which surprised us because there seemed to be so little resistance in front; but we did not complain.

On 2 August C Squadron probed south for the Etouvy/La Graverie area, where an enemy force reacted vigorously to our approach. There was a deep screen of trees between SHQ and our leading troops closing in on the place, so that we could not see what was happening. I offered on squadron net to put down 95 mm support by map reference, asking Jimmy Grimstone in the forward troop to correct my shooting by observation.

I concentrated on the tips Tony Venner had given me about the gun. The first round was loaded – all ammunition was high explosive (HE), there were no armour-piercing rounds – and I estimated the range from the map reference Jimmy had given. For both the gunner and me it was our first firing of a 95 mm. The loader/operator tapped the gunner's shoulder, and we were ready.

'Fire!'

The gun recoiled, ran out, the expelled shell-case fell through the chute to the turret floor. Smoke abounded. Would the explosive-packed projectile land among our own tanks, on some innocent Norman dwelling or anywhere near an enemy position? We waited, then Jimmy's voice came through on radio.

'Sorry. Couldn't see where it landed at all.'

I corrected boldly, reducing the range and keeping the same alignment. We fired again.

'Oh yes!' There was satisfaction in Jimmy's tone. 'That looks about the right sort of area. A few more like that ought to shift something.'

Beginner's luck! We carried on firing. Suddenly right above our heads crackled the black menace of an enemy airburst, his tribute to the effectiveness of our shooting. While the 88 was airbursting us, it could not fire in an anti-tank role at our forward troops. We closed down to avoid becoming casualties, and maintained our delivery. The turret became a chamber of smoke and cordite fumes. Then the operator remembered that this tank was fitted with a small extractor fan for just this occasion. He pointed to it. I reached across and switched on. It functioned. Slowly the interior began to clear, air coming in through the hatch joints.

Jimmy reported they were closing in. Some enemy were surrendering. An anti-tank gun had been destroyed. We could cease support fire.

Squadron HQ stayed no longer than was unavoidable in the area of houses where civilian rejoicing followed the forward troops' success. It was not long before Big Mac was hustling the whole squadron east towards La Bistière and the main road that came from Caen via Villers-Bocage to go gently downhill here to the outskirts of the town called Vire.

The leading troops turned onto this main and were well on the way to the Y (i.e. forked) roads north of the town before they came under anti-tank gunfire from the area of the junction. Jimmy and the other forward troop leader, Lieutenant Saxby, returned HE and machine-gun fire into the general area, but every time they tried to move forward, an enemy gun fired again. The position was evidently well protected and concealed. The troops waited, off the road, and watched, firing at intervals but with as little effect as before. We were not to know that this was an example of Hauptgruppenführer Hausser's 7th Army policy that day to concentrate on holding major road junctions, in the confident belief that the solid hedges of the *bocage* would frustrate Allied tank movement off the roads. Certainly our troops were not finding a way round the junction across country.

On the far side of La Bistière recce troop was soon to report seeing a detachment of enemy infantry. Back where we had come from, B Squadron was exploring past Etouvy along the more direct route to the Y roads and Vire, but they reported opposition stiffening.

C Squadron HQ was halted at the more southerly junction of the lateral road with the main, near La Bistière and to the south of the little ridge, so that we could see well down the main road to the haze forming above our partly concealed forward troops. There was an abundance of tree and bush cover down there. The 95 mms could waste a deal of ammunition plastering an expanse like that.

SHQ was still in the same location when the A Squadron column appeared along the road from the north. Their new major came forward and conferred.

I reckoned the Oxford tactical course would have counselled Mac that, if his troops were unable either to pass the road junction or to locate the opposition, he should ask his accompanying artillery OP to put down twenty-five-pounder concentrations on the general area, and to get his tanks forward before the concentrations ceased. Mac's problem – and it could hardly have endeared the Oxford course or me to him – was that the divisional artillery were deployed with a first priority to the armoured and infantry brigade groups, and there was no OP officer with C Squadron on the British right flank.

Mac muttered about this to himself until I suggested he

might get Alastair to radio regiment for some air support such as I had witnessed on Hill 112 in June. It was a fine day, we had seen the occasional fighter aircraft cruising around on its own initiative, so it must be good flying weather.

Alastair said there was no harm in asking, and Mac said: 'Do it!'

Alastair was studiedly polite to regiment, who were predictably non-committal. Within an hour we had a cab-rank of four rocket-firing Typhoons circling us in the blue, blue sky just looking for an indicator of what to dive on. The forward troops had been cautioned to display their identifying yellow fluorescent strips on tank top. Jimmy fired some smoke shells into the concealing cover around the approach to the Y roads. The planes had to circle several times before the smoke matured sufficiently to be seen. Then they went into their drill for delivering the rockets.

The whole squadron – and A as well – watched spellbound and motionless. Four screaming crescendos, eight pulverizing explosions. The Typhoons pulled out of their dive one by one, re-formed and returned to base. It was done.

Mac cackled down his microphone for the front troop to move a tank. As soon as one moved, enemy positions came to life, firing everything they had. The squadron was back to square one.

It was evening before the leading troops found they could make progress again. The defenders had evidently pulled out without waiting for dark, guns and all – except for one, hit and wrecked, abandoned beside the Y roads – and so quietly! All tanks of C Squadron moved line ahead down the road to Vire.

Where a road joined the main from the left was a wide clearing, which enabled the two leading troops and SHQ to see as far as the side road's first bend. Down it towards us on collision course came a column of lorries and trucks, fast-moving, enemy. Tanks halted, guns traversing left.

'What are you waiting for?' On squadron net Big Mac lashed us all. 'Let 'em have it!'

Besa machine-guns and the HE of 75 mms spurted out into the path of 'soft' vehicles. Some went off on one bank, some onto the other, a few burst into flame on the crown of the road. One or two trucks attempted to turn about. All were caught in the appalling volume of tank-fire. Field-grey and camouflaged figures leapt down and ran for any cover, some with their clothes blazing, others mown down in the road or into the ditch.

My gunner and operator looked up at me expectantly. I knew I had given no fire order. I shook my head at them. The 95 mm was not needed. I was working out from the map where the enemy vehicles had come from. They had clearly been oblivious of the presence of British tanks across their route – after all, we had only just arrived that far. The lorries had possibly just supplied or reinforced units opposing the advance of our own brigade groups south-east towards a ridge just north of the Vire–Vassy road. They would have been expecting a clear run through Vire, an important communication junction for the 7th Army so far. Alastair's recent information from regiment quoted armoured car reports that the town had earlier been clear of enemy but was now being frantically fortified with roadblocks and supporting trenches.

Mac ordered cease-fire and resumption of our southward push. Parts of Vire were now visible under a faint evening mist and the fading light, seemingly terraced up a north-east facing slope. With the same two troops in the lead, we moved on again, over a small river, across a railway line. Anti-tank fire opened up on us suddenly from the right rear. Solid projectiles whined past the line of Cromwells. One seared red-hot across the road surface between my tank and the one in front of it. Another did the same further along. The shots were coming from north of Vire, precise origin unlocated, not short-range.

Mac halted the squadron again. All traversed towards the new threat, beginning exploratory fire. The approaching dusk defied our seeing any effect from our shooting, which had scarcely begun when Alastair passed orders to Mac, who abruptly called on us all to cease fire and turn back the way we had come. Whatever our aim had been only five minutes ago – to capture Vire without infantry support? – it was all off now.

We trundled back to the La Bistière junction, then west almost to La Graverie to harbour. Watching the Y roads was delegated to a patrol from recce troop. The explanation given was that higher HQ had reaffirmed the inclusion of Vire all along in the American sector of advance. At the same time there was no information about how near our US neighbours were to Vire. I uncharitably thought it could have been they who had just poured anti-tank fire at us, and missed. Regiment also failed to pass us the day's most significant item of news, that on our neighbours' right, the American VII Corps had captured Mortain, some thirteen miles further south. The net had begun to close around the enemy, and he could be expected to hit back hard.

In ignorant bliss of the morrow's nasty surprises, C Squadron welcomed the arrival of its echelon in the dark, took in rations and water and replenished its considerable expenditure of ammunition. That night B Squadron, located further forward and to our right, was stalked continuously by enemy infantry, who used mortars, grenades and bazookas to cause them casualties in and out of the tanks, and to keep them sleepless. On the left, nearer La Bistière, A Squadron experienced more exploratory stalking. Yet in C, having been told that, following our day leading the regiment we should be in reserve on the morrow, we settled down and slept like tops, in which happy state, if any enemy patrols came near, they left us. Our line sentries heard nothing.

At daylight on 3 August we were clearly on the regimental right, albeit in reserve. Our troops faced right to take care of the British flank again, but also to watch for signs of *los Americanos*.

A Squadron set out to work its way south on side roads to the east of the Caen–Vire road. B was to feel its way forward towards the outskirts of Vire again but on an axis further west than A's. With us in C all was quiet: it was just a pleasantly hot day.

After a late lunch I slid under the back of the tank for an hour's siesta. I was awakened somewhere near five o'clock by the sound of Big Mac stomping along asking for Captain Jones. My crew would have wakened me gently but he brushed past them to reach a hand under the tank's rear, ostensibly to shake me. As I had woken already, I grasped his hand to facilitate extricating myself, blinking at our large squadron commander in the afternoon sunlight as he advanced a map board in his other hand and poured out his alarming news at me.

'Enemy counter-attack coming in, with Tiger tanks!'

'Where?'

He gestured with two fingers up the general line of the road from Vire, the route back that we had followed last night.

'They're coming up towards this ridge. More or less into the middle of the regiment by the look of it.' His forefinger scrubbed the map to indicate which ridge, parallel with the east–west road La Graverie–La Bistière and south of it. 'I want you to reconnoitre troop positions where they'll be able to get a good shoot at the enemy as he comes over the ridge.'

'Shall I take the scoutcar?'

'No time. Go in your tank, and get off at once.'

A tank on its own is no tank, Oxford had said. And a 95 mm gun had no AP for Tigers.

'What about HQ troop sergeant for escort?'

'No, you're on your own.' Then, 'We'll be almost on your tail.'

The crew had heard it all. We mounted up and went, out of the field, left along the east–west road, about half-way before we halted first time. I checked out the approaches to two troop positions and then a third, all on the slope to the south. They gave a choice of cover and a field of fire up to the ridge.

I encoded the co-ordinates and radio'd back, saying I should next report positions for a reserve sub-unit and for control (HQ) in depth, afterwards seeking a fourth forward position on what would then be left flank. The reserve troop and SHQ, I reckoned, needed to be behind the hedge on the left (north) side of the road, where there were gaps for firing through and also a couple of lines of covered withdrawal if necessary. Moving on, I passed data for these positions as I found them. Only the left forward troop position remained to be identified.

The turn off the lateral road connecting with the main to Vire came into view in front. Once we turned right onto it, I envisaged probing gently towards the point where it crossed the ridge before descending to join the main. I hoped to find a position off the road to the right which might also afford a troop cover for withdrawing directly down to the lateral road, a feature that had not been obvious as we came along the lateral road itself.

As we approached the junction, I told the crew what we were going to do. It would be an acute-angle turn to the right, probably needing first gear. The driver went down his gear box to get the tightest turning circle, four to three, three to two.

I recall feeling satisfaction at what we had achieved in such a short time. On 'A' set we could hear the squadron moving out to take up the positions reported. We slowed towards the threshold of the junction, and I could feel my adrenalin working with anticipation of completing the trickiest part of the assignment. I had no inkling that I was about to make a serious blunder.

The tank was almost at the corner when I heard a number of guns firing and felt two projectiles zip past the turret. If I had had any doubt about my perception, the operator disappeared precipitately below hatches. Staying head out, I spoke sharply into the microphone on intercom.

'Driver, speed it up! We're being shot at!'

I could hear the enemy's quick-firing machine-guns as well now. The counter-attack must have reached a point just over the brow of the road from us.

Faithfully, the driver put his foot down on the accelerator instead of changing down one more gear to first. He lugged simultaneously full strength on the right tiller bar, for the acute turn was upon us. The tank eased round as she would in second, not tight enough. Up she went onto the crown of the main road, skidded across and down the other side. There was at most a three-foot grass shoulder and then, deceptively deep, a ditch. A tank's length and we were in it, all twenty-eight tons of us, the port beam coming to rest along its far side, the tank at an angle near to 45 degrees, the driving sprockets threshing under 600 brake horsepower to no avail at all, stuck.

'Sorry, sir!'

'My fault! I should have kept quiet and you'd have been all right. Try her in reverse.'

He did; same effect.

'I think both tracks are off.'

I heaved myself up at the angle of the heavy list, but I had to clamber right out and lean over to confirm he was right. As I got back, a shell burst on the opposite verge of the road, slightly in front of the tank.

'Keep in cover. Switch off engine.'

I reported our indisposition on 'A' set, telling where I was and about the enemy shooting, suggesting the left sub-unit call in on me for guidance in finding his own fire position.

On intercom I asked the gunner what he could see through his telescope by hand-traversing left and right and varying his elevation. It sounded hard work for him, traversing right against gravity. Eventually he said he either saw sky or foliage. There was no way he could make the gun point at the road where it disappeared over the ridge. The co-driver reported that, whatever he did with the hull Besa, his telescope saw only plant life.

'So stand by to bale out. Get your small kits ready.'

Back along the lateral road a lone troop was approaching us and the corner. I took off headphones, planted both feet on the inside turret ring. Leaning across the unlevel top, I signed one finger at the leading tank, first gear. Reaching for my microphone, on intercom:

'All ready to move? There's a gateway with a bit of cover and a stone wall twenty yards back on the left. I'll join you there.'

The troop leader's tank came round steadily. I moved a foot up to the cupola rim to push myself further across the turret, then decided I should only be blocking the operator's exit. I hauled clear until I was perched on the right running-board, ready to shout at the new arrival.

Nothing had fired at him until he halted his machine beside mine. Then an HE shell burst on the road behind him, just as the second tank was making its turn. At least the shots were not armour-piercing. That probably meant the enemy was unable to see us yet and was firing HE at our noise, that the projectiles whizzing past my turret at the turn might not have been visually aimed at it.

I told the troop leader where I thought he should look for his fire position, off to the right before his turrets could show above the ridge. I said the enemy must be close on the other side. He nodded grimly, spoke into his mike. The tank surged forward in first gear, then eased to a cautious pace. It was a hundred yards or more to the summit, not a steep slope.

My crew came out with their haversacks.

'Don't hang about, sir. We'll be by the gate.'

I got back into the turret, put my codes into the haversack, checked binoculars were still round my neck, took the map out of the board, folded it smaller, stuffed it inside my shirt with my identity discs and the sweat. On 'A' set I told Mac there was nothing I could do where I was, so I should return to him on foot. I unlocked and detuned the radio set, switched off and contorted across the inside of the turret to reach just behind the driver's compartment and turn off the master-switch. Then I climbed back and out, to leave the vehicle.

As my head emerged above cupola level, one of the troop tanks was reversing down the slope towards me at maximum revs. A shell burst on the road beside mine and behind his. He carried on down to the junction.

I moved out fast, down across the ditch, which was dry, back along its fringe and into the gateway by the stone wall where the others in our crew were waiting. To my surprise, they were being harangued by a civilian in smock and beret, same uniform as the one with the bicycle back at the long wood.

'You must fight the Boche!' What did it look as if we were doing? 'You will not win by leaving your tank!'

Another shell exploded nearby, and I reflected that he might be right to the extent that the tank would give protection from bursts. I prepared the crew to sprint to the far side of the road in a bunch, five of us together. The peasant's persistence was making me cross. I was already fed up with myself about the tank, unfightable without having been hit. The thing could be hauled out and made functional again within an hour, by whichever side got to it first. Before we left, I mustered my best school French to make some response to this idiot who thought we were running away.

'N'ayez pas peur. Nous gagnerons cette guerre!' – 'Don't be afraid. We shall win this war!'

'Oh, vive l'Angleterre!' – 'Long live England!'

As we ducked across the road, I fancied he watched us with derision. Anyway it was mutual.

It seemed a long way along the northern verge of the lateral road before we reached SHQ and the reserve troop. Big Mac was hunched over his microphone in touch with the dozen tanks up the slope to the south. He showed no sign of wanting to speak to me. My crew rested down in cover, and I went over to Alastair to find out what news had been reaching him on regimental net.

That hour or so's sleep of mine had missed me out on a mountain of events. On side roads A Squadron had reached the railway line just north of Vire, the one we had crossed the night before when we came under anti-tank fire. A was also in contact with the infantry brigade holding ground between exclusive La Bistière and the Perrier Ridge overlooking the Vire–Vassy road. It was through the no man's land just south of that area that groups of Panzer grenadiers and Tiger tanks began to appear later in the day, and to engage A Squadron from its exposed flank.

On the regimental right front, B Squadron had moved

down the main road against disarmingly less opposition than we had experienced yesterday, and reached the Y junction. In the afternoon they had just received a report from a civilian who purported to be in the French Resistance, that Vire was now clear of German troops, when they rubbed their eyes to see a column of Tiger tanks with accompanying infantry debouch from the town to move steadily north astride the main road to Villers-Bocage and Caen. B Squadron had taken cover off and further up the road on higher ground, and watched.

How much detail regiment had given at the time was not clear, but the facts were that the 9th SS Panzer Division, disengaged from the Canadian sector and coming from east of the Orne, had been ordered to report to the German 7th Army well west of our position, and to restore the line where Patton's Army had torrented through into Brittany. The Panzers had taken punishment from the air most of their way, especially crossing the Orne, but now finding the British contesting their line of advance they at once grouped aggressively to engage us.

That, shortly before Mac had come over to waken me, one of our troops in C had reported seeing American infantry at last moving south towards Vire, was no particular help now, because they had been well clear of our dispersed regimental position.

Improving on the day before, artillery OP officers were with both A and B squadrons. When the enemy appeared from Vire, B's commander logically asked for a divisional shoot on the Tiger pack. It happened that on this fine August day division had Typhoons on ten-minute call. Someone argued that rockets were more effective against Tigers than twenty-five pounder fire, which was true. So a spotter plane was sent up to tell the Typhoons just where to dive, another improvement on arrangements of the day before.

German groundfire then shot down the spotter plane, and the Typhoons failed to locate the target. This was not so surprising, because 9th SS, seeing aircraft about again, took full advantage of the ample tree cover to the west of the main road.

While the artillery had held off to let the aircraft perform, the enemy force had worked steadily north until it was virtually in among the troops of B Squadron. An artillery shoot was no longer a practicable option.

From tree cluster to bush clump, from hedgerow to *bocage* hedgerow, B Squadron tanks had engaged the enemy force. Their armour-piercing shots were predictably ineffective against Tiger frontal armour, but when they fired at the flanks, the solidarity of the *bocage* walls in which the hedges had been rooted for centuries broke the force of the AP before it ever reached the Tigers. This was a day in which failure to equip the regiment with the one-in-four Sherman Fireflies, mounting seventeen-pounder guns, as accorded to the armoured regiments, made all the difference.

B Squadron lost three tanks before the colonel ordered withdrawal to block the main road further north. In withdrawing, the tanks came under long-range fire from the other Tiger force that had appeared between A Squadron and the infantry brigade positions, and B lost three more tanks. At this juncture A Squadron was also ordered to pull back. No wonder the colonel had called C Squadron out of reserve to man the ridge!

This was the position reached as Alastair concluded his résumé of events to me behind the hedge along the lateral road. SHQ and the reserve troop watched the area of patchy cover along the ridge over which the Waffen SS would surely come.

In the next fifteen minutes sounds of battle came nearer. On regimental net both A and B reported losing more tanks, and our own had casualties among its dozen up the hill, surviving crews beginning to arrive in the field where we stood.

Somewhere up that slope to the south also, RHQ itself was in trouble. Alastair and I heard the RHQ troop leader in his excitement give a fire order on 'A' set. The remarkable thing was that his gunner not only heard the order but carried it out. Still using the command net, the same voice became ecstatic about a bull's-eye, soon adding with incredulity: 'You've brewed him!'

Big Mac screwed himself round in his cupola and surveyed the growing number of tankless crews. He shouted down at me: 'Keith, you're doing no good here. Better get these dismounted crews back to the echelon before you're all shot to bits!'

He was right, of course. I shouted back that I would rejoin him as soon as I could collect another tank. He turned back to look up towards the ridge. I got on with the evacuation task, dividing all those on foot into small parties. I gave them an assembly area in a copse we could just see at the distant corner of our huge field. They were to wait for me there. The parties moved off at intervals along alternate sides of the perimeter so that they would present minimal targets. Already 'overs' from the fight up the hill, including bursts from quick-firing machine-guns, were enlivening our rural environment.

Alastair had some insoluble trouble with his tank. He spoke to Mac, then said he and his crew would like to join me in going back. All parties were away, my own crew included, so Alastair and I followed his four along the west perimeter.

As we came level with a gap from the road, RHQ began to drive into the field, having withdrawn from their too-lively position up the hill. The RHQ troop leader's Cromwell led them in. George Davies dismounted inside the gap to direct vehicles left and right along the perimeter hedge.

Spotting Alastair and me, he was busting to tell us how a French peasant had set him up to train his gun on a hedge gap in the field they had just left, and then stepped back to beckon a Tiger through the gap, giving George a point-blank lateral shot – the one we heard on regimental net – which had brewed the Tiger. As he directed RHQ to its new resting-place, George was dancing his elation on the resilient grass. I left Alastair chatting to him. I could sense big trouble building up, and I had a job to do.

I had seen the colonel come in, sitting on the front of his

tank with one arm over the gun barrel, as if he were giving driving instruction without using the intercom. He looked very tired. I saw the medical officer and the padre sharing a half-track. George directed them along the perimeter where I was going, further back from the road towards the corner with the copse. Another half-track was being shared by the technical adjutant and Ernie Ehrenfeld, who had succeeded Alastair as intelligence officer. I also noticed the signals officer, who had joined the regiment with me from the West Kents' armoured car unit a year before. All this vehicle-sharing: RHQ must have had trouble.

When I caught up with where the MO's vehicle had come to rest, he was already attending to wounded whom he must have brought with him in it. Seeing me, he asked if I would like to be a good chap and pop back to the field they had just left, because they had abandoned another half-track there, and it contained several bags of their shell dressings. I grinned at his unreality, asked if he could hear the machine-guns of the Panzer grenadiers who had now taken possession of his shell dressings, adding as casually as I could that I had to see survivors of knocked-out tanks back to the echelon to fight again another day.

The MO went on with his task, looking over his shoulder at me to say calmly: 'All right, Keith. See you anon.'

Padre Lang was reassuring: they had quite a few big ones with them and would manage.

I had moved fewer than a dozen steps beyond the half-track and heard some guns firing in quick succession, when their high-explosive shells landed among us. I dived for the foot of the mud wall bearing the hedge. The ground was heaving. The bursts were ear-splitting.

As the concentration persisted, day turned into local night. Flame spurts pierced the murk of flying earth and fragments in the choking smoke. I had pictured the enemy environment at Bras and in the Tiger wood; now it was my turn to be at the receiving-end of 'fire for effect', first-hand experience that far outlasted the impact of the Moaning

Minnies of Hill 112. To think that I had volunteered for the infantry, was it five years ago?

My tummy was surely trying to dig a hole in the springy turf, while with each fresh explosion I was bounced up into the lethal night, only to flop down again and resume my phantasied digging-in. I fastened fingers in roots to hold me down, to no avail. I ought to have been deafened, but still I could hear the guns firing with the next load, before its predecessor had subsided. I asked myself aloud, would they never stop? How much longer would it take counter-battery fire to locate and neutralize? But of course, who was there with a net to call for counter-battery fire? Through it all, the other sounds I heard were of human agony.

By the time there was a pause, I could no longer trust it. No one moved at first, because it would surely begin again. Everyone alive was coughing into the unreal silence. The cries of pain had become more muffled moans before the smoke could even start to clear. Peering ahead, I began to see that the mud wall just a yard in front of my head was entirely demolished. I wriggled forward, got to my knees, crawled two steps into the field. Was I really unhurt?

The body I now loomed over was very still. A gash, that might have come from a two-handed sword of ancient times, had opened up the thorax from beside the neck to below the waist. I thought the head moved. A tight-mesh personal camouflage net attached to the steel helmet half covered the face. I lifted it fearfully aside, recognizing him, the first driver to let me practise belting his Centaur training tank about the Yorkshire Wolds last year. Now he was dead, or near to death, beyond human help.

Replacing the net I forced myself to look, briefly enough, at the next three bodies nearby, before crawling back to the MO's half-track. He had already resumed his task of dressing wounds. I said something silly, like: 'Sorry about the shell dressings.'

'We'll be all right, Keith. You'd better see who you can get out of here on two feet before the next lot starts up.'

'Will you and Padre come? There's not much you can do for those I've just seen, and the Panzer grenadiers may be here any time.'

'We're staying put. Those I can't help, Padre will pray for.'

I remembered how in Britain he, Captain G.H.V. Clark RAMC, had refused the issue of a pistol.

'You take care of the walkers, Keith. Good luck!'

I reached the end of the field before more explosions began back where I had been. A second lieutenant I ought to have recognized was propped against the corner wall. The assembly area was on the other side, in the copse. I addressed him:

'Are you hurt?'

He smiled weakly. 'Don't think so. Just couldn't get over.'

I made a stirrup of two hands, helped him up. Over he went, other hands on the far side pulling him through the thick hedge and down into its lee. I followed, suddenly feeling tottery myself.

Most of the dismounted crews had made it, stragglers still coming in. Many displayed blackened patches of clothing and skin, as I fancy I did too. My second lieutenant was now propped against this side of the wall. Another one was bleeding gently from under one ear, his arms supported on the shoulders of a trooper and a sergeant, who said the officer was deaf but could walk. Alastair, who had somehow arrived before me, stood wiping his spectacles. Others were seated or lying down, recovering, but most were on their feet, looking at me, keen to be gone.

As I hauled my map out of its sweaty and now dust-permeated hiding-place, I realized I was the only one in the party to have one. I opened it out and looked at it, located where we were. I had no idea where the echelon was, and Alastair could not remember its reporting location on regimental net all day. I guessed at the kind of area we needed to aim at and worked out on the map how we could approach it under reasonable cover.

'This wooded area will give us cover for a mile back, so we can keep together unless we're shot at. Move as quietly as you can and keep your voices down. All set?'

Over thirty of us moved off. I attached my haversack to the back of my belt, both hands free. Someone had put a field dressing on the subaltern's ear. I fancied he was not the only one who was hurt, but no one was admitting to a wound of consequence. We walked slowly. From inside the fringe of the wood we had a good view across succeeding crops and pastures under the evening sun to the left.

Beyond the mile, the wood thinned out before resuming in a more obviously north direction. People asked if we could rest. I called a halt in a clearing. Already the rustling and the bird-song of the country had reasserted themselves. I leaned my back against a tree, checked that my Smith & Wesson had rounds in five of its six chambers, put it back in its holster, turned my attention to the contents of an escape pack I had carried in my battledress blouse since the phase of the long wood.

The ampoule of morphine I had used on the trooper grenade casualty was the only thing removed from the pack all this time. I had not replenished it. There was an empty rubber water-pouch to hang round the neck, a sheet of tablets to chlorinate doubtful water, another to counter the taste of chlorine. I had left my army water-bottle on the tank. A third sheet, of benzedrine tablets (used to keep a tired escaper, or pilot, awake), I intuitively viewed with abhorrence. But that was not all.

I fingered the small button compass, which pointed the way we were going almost as accurately as the larger prismatic one in my belt-pouch. What I treasured most, and always shall, was the folded linen escape map that showed air crews how to make for a neutral country from any part of occupied Europe. I opened it out to enjoy the contour-coloured print on either side: Berlin–Munich–Troyes–Amsterdam, or Switzerland–Marseilles, with an inset of the Ardennes on a better scale. Alastair watched me savouring it. He was evidently sufficiently recovered to twit me in his soft Scots accent.

'When it comes to maps, Keith, you're quite a baby!'

At that moment I noticed that my prized escape map nowhere featured Normandy. I folded it safely away.

'What amazes me is how I escaped in that mighty stonk back there, without a scratch. People near me were …'

Alastair could see well now that his specs were clean. 'Have you looked at your beret?'

I took it off. In the crease that ran from near the regimental badge towards the crown of the head was a rent, not large and almost closed over again. But it was there: it marked the passage of a sliver of metal, which had gone in on one side of the crease, scraped on my abundant hair and made egress on the far side. I poked my little finger in through the first rent and out again beyond the crease, made a face, replaced my beret and called the party to order. We must move on.

In less than another mile we could see where soon the wood was going to come to an end. We should have to cross open ground. But what was that to the left? Perhaps half a mile off, across a large open field of grass that was to reach almost up to my bottom, regularly spaced along a very low hedge, were four armoured vehicles propping up their camouflage nets, guns pointing south.

'Do you agree they're ours?' I asked Alastair.

'I'd not like to say at this distance. Left my binoculars on the tank.'

I felt for mine, always round my neck. They were gone. I knew I had brought them from the tank, would not have taken their strap from round my neck at any point since. That stonk had much to answer for.

'Why do you say they're ours?' Alastair was challenging now.

'Regularly spaced, guns pointing south, bad camouflage.'

'I hope you're right,' he said. 'We have to cross open ground soon anyway. They can't fail to see us. What are you going to do?'

'Keep the party along the fringe here in cover while I go forward to make sure. Once I'm close enough to them, I'll identify myself and wave you all to follow me.'

'And if they're enemy?' The Scots always consider every possibility.

'You all wait here till dark. I play Red Indians through the long grass to rejoin you.'

So I went, undoing my neckerchief on the way. It was a torn piece of yellow fluorescent cloth that suited the August weather better than a necktie. When I thought the crews of the armoured vehicles had noticed me, I waved the cloth as I walked forward, in what I thought to be a reassuring gesture, because only the Allies had yellow fluorescent cloth! My torn piece was admittedly neither clean nor as fluorescent as it had once been.

At 300 yards I could identify the vehicles as M.10 tank-destroyers – 76 mm anti-tank guns self-propelled on a North American tank chassis bearing a distinctive open-topped turret – so they were either American – or British-manned. At 200 I could see through the camouflage nets to the blue-and-red vehicle flashes of the Royal Artillery. Two crew sitting above one turret were in unmistakably British battledress. They must be anti-tank gunners from our own division.

At 150 yards I waved my yellow cloth some more, halted to shout the name of my regiment, saying we were crews of knocked-out tanks and there were quite a few of us. Feeling sure I was heard and understood, I turned to wave Alastair & Co to come out of the wood, before resuming my lone advance. One of the crew on turret was a sergeant. At the foot of the vehicle was an artillery lieutenant, who must have taken in my every word.

It was the sight of my companions surging forward from the wood, I realized afterwards, that alarmed the artillery subaltern into action. He called up to the turret: 'Sergeant, pick that man off!'

The sergeant had a Sten gun, for which I was the only man in range. He cocked the Sten, came into the aim, pointing it unmistakably at me.

Even then I could have dived into the grass, but the windy subaltern would have turned whatever full-size machine-gun he had on the rest of the crews following me. How could I show I was not German? I kept walking, took a deep breath and shouted, fit for the drill square, 'Don't be a fucking idiot! Put that Sten down, Sergeant!'

He came out of the aim, still pointing the thing at me. The lieutenant drew his pistol and walked forward, putting the weapon away again when I shouted some more.

'I've got at least one wounded officer in this party. Can you whistle up some stretcher-bearers or something?'

He called to his radio-operator before turning back to me.

'Sorry, Captain. Can't be too careful. Don't the SS wear black hats, too? Has the counter-attack petered out?'

'I doubt it. At least it hasn't come this a way ... yet. Better keep your chaps alert. We could have done with your muzzle velocity down there an hour ago.'

Alastair told how George had bagged his Tiger. An RA jeep ambulance drove up. The second lieutenant with the bleeding ear was lifted onto its upper stretcher and strapped down. I leaned over him as he was fully conscious, looked him full in the eyes and nodded to say he would soon be all right now. He grasped my hand firmly for a moment. Then I stepped down and he was driven off.

I thanked the AT lieutenant for getting the jeep and said I must walk the main party back to echelon for more tanks.

'I can show you the way to divisional HQ, and you can ask your way from there.'

Alastair was happy for us to walk to Div. HQ. It was dark when we arrived. A guide was produced to see the other second lieutenant and the whole party on to A echelon. Alastair and I were invited to tarry awhile with friends at Div. He was teetotal but I accepted an enormous pink gin with my wad of bread, butter and jam. It was all I needed for an abreaction: loosening of the tongue. Before long I was entertaining an understanding GOC with my animated account of the SS assault on our under-gunned yeomanry, asking him what he was doing to support them in their agony.

It was not until well after we had reached the echelon that pieces of news began to add up, in fact not until near mid-morning of the following day, 4 August. Having deluged HQ's adopted harbour with high explosive on the 3rd, the SS battle group paused. It would be gratifying to say that C Squadron, in the fire positions I had reconnoitred for them, held the line, and so they did. At least, if they had not been there, the Panzers might have pushed their luck further. More probably the enemy just deemed it prudent to stay put for the night. They were in possession of the ridge, from which they shelled and mortared the field I had found for C Squadron HQ that RHQ joined, spasmodically all night.

In casualties, besides the four who had been mortally wounded so close to me in that field before I left it, six others were killed, including the technical adjutant (Captain Cooke-Hurle) and the intelligence officer (Ernie Ehrenfeld), whose shared half-track received a direct hit. Altogether three subalterns and ten others were wounded. From the forward squadrons three more subalterns and fourteen others were missing.

The yeomanry echelon was run by the warrant officers, and very well they did it: I had felt cared for from the moment I arrived. A rum ration was put into my hand, which went down well on top of Div. HQ's pink gin, and I slept content until the sunlight twinkled anew and the birdies twittered.

Today I was grateful to be able to write to the woman in my life. I took paper and envelope out of the haversack – but what to say? 'We've just had a close call'? I was not allowed to say that for a fortnight anyway. 'I am safe at the moment'? That would not do either. If I said I was spending time with the warrant officers, she might think I was hurt, had lost my tank, no. I could hardly say, 'Wish you were here', so I might say, 'Wish I were with you.' I settled for saying how much I loved her, as I had in countless previous letters. It was still true.

There was no question, the WOs said, of the regiment's being able to receive replacement tanks and crews until dark that night. What the echelon had taken forward while we were all walking back to it the evening before was something the sergeant-majors were not saying much about. I inferred that a mixed-load lorry and a water cart had ventured as far as RHQ and C Squadron in between shellings. A and B Squadrons were isolated and unsafe to approach, although it was hoped they might have had some help through the infantry brigade. Having no infantry with them, the isolates were stalked by SS patrols all night. Some eight tanks of A were lost to bazooka shots, while over at B, Captain Wilkins mysteriously disappeared into the dark.

In daylight the regimental net was heard to order the harassed A and B Squadrons to withdraw towards friends on their left (infantry brigade). Two more tanks were bazooka'd as they withdrew, two more officers to die of their wounds. The single remaining troop of B was put under the command of what remained of A after its night of being bazooka'd. It has been said that a troop of seventeen-pounder anti-tank guns got through to join them. With this force, A Squadron was to prevent further enemy movement north or north-east of La Bistière, which was after all very near the point where my 95 mm tank lay helpless in a ditch.

Somewhere else in the tangle of small groups of friend or foe that stalked each other or were stalked from one high-hedged field to another, night and day, was Major Courage, B squadron commander since his predecessor was wounded south of Caen, with one other tank. To us, back in the peace of the echelon, it was a day of activity we could only imagine, because the infrequent and cautious messages on the RSM's regimental wavelength gave very little comprehensive information. Only much later we heard that the infantry brigade had mounted a company strength attack on La Bistière, but it sustained casualties and failed.

One thing we certainly did not learn was that 4 August was the day on which Hitler ordered Field Marshal von Kluge to collect in every available Panzer division and smash through from the Vire–Mortain area – virtually under our feet – to the coast at Avranches, so cutting off the Americans in Brittany. And Hitler did not know that the British advance was already intercepting three of those Panzer divisions (9th and 10th SS and 21st), and so fully committing them that they never took part in the thrust to the coast.

In the evening dark of the 4th I returned to our uncertain regimental situation, in a new 95 mm gun close-support tank, as well as other replacement tanks and crews. We drove into C Squadron's new field, which seemed very close to the old one.

I had had a lovely wash all over that day, cleaned my teeth properly more than once, drunk sergeant-major tea, changed my underclothes and exchanged my battledress for my waterproof flying-suit, my brown infantry boots for my pull-on flying-boots, just to have a change of togs. So I was feeling almost relaxed, alert for whatever the night had to offer, conscious of my infantry training in night work.

Big Mac was not a bit pleased to see us. I wondered how much sleep he had had since we left him twenty-six hours earlier. All the old squadron was on tenterhooks for enemy night patrols, and the unavoidable noise of our arrival drove them mad until we had added our tanks to the tight laager well clear of the mud hedge-walls, and killed engines.

In the eerie silence that followed, Jimmy Grim' and I stood close to the perimeter wall on the most likely side for a patrol approach, he with his pistol out and I with a grenade, straining our ears to identify sounds on the other side. What was different since I left was that a detachment of Royal Engineers had joined the squadron for the night as an infantry surrogate. I wondered if my rash conversation with our good-natured general had produced this extra support, or whether he would have sent the sappers along anyway.

Jimmy had been manning a rear-link radio and acting 2 I/C as well. Alastair had not returned with me to the squadron, being wanted back at RHQ to pick up the function of RIO again, now that Ernie was dead.

In C Squadron we heard enemy patrols twice during the night, but they were reconnoitring quietly and made no attempt to molest us. I stayed on my feet most of the night, hoping Big Mac would allow himself some sleep. I had to respect him for seeing the squadron through, and single-handed. We stood to for an hour before dawn, but all was serene by full daylight. 9th SS must have been tired too.

As the sun warmed up, regimental net gave Mac his orders. An infantry division was coming into the general area next to the sector down to Vire, now firmly the responsibility of the American 1st Army. The regiment would soon withdraw into divisional reserve. C Squadron was given a map reference for a new harbour area, and I was to depart at once by scoutcar to reconnoitre it.

'While you're there, find a water supply and as soon as we're installed, get some baths organized for the squadron,' Mac told me. 'Hot ones!'

I went. The scoutcar sped along the lateral road that I had followed on another reconnaissance – by tank – only the day before yesterday. At the acute road junction I halted the driver to look across at my abandoned tank, still there, still helpless in the dry ditch. Were all the stories about prompt German tank-recovery exaggerated, or did they simply not want another Cromwell?

Everything was quiet. Was the enemy still there in the La Bistière area, just over the brow of the hill?

I looked steadily at the tank. Two of the running-board bins were open and smouldering. The tank had been pilfered, vandalized, perhaps hit by mortar or shell-fire or just hit in the bins by machine-gun tracer. Something was hanging out of a smouldering bin, a cavalry-length greatcoat. I jumped down, walked over to the tank, lugged at the greatcoat. Mine! Big patches had been burned out of it; only the top half with the epaulettes and the six pips was still serviceable. I tossed it back on the vehicle and returned to the scoutcar.

We hurtled up the main road to the new harbour area. I checked there were no mines, worked out the best main entry point, where to put the tanks within the total space, which part to keep vacant for visiting replenishment vehicles, access for them, where to organize baths if the echelon could get water and the means of heating it up that day. Then I looked at the map for a local water-supply in case the echelon failed to make it before dark. In a farm about a mile away across fields, a well was marked.

I radio'd Mac to say I had checked out our new estate, fixed a rendezvous point with him, on the main road some 200 yards north-east of my immobile tank. The scoutcar moved back there to wait, turning round to face the new harbour ready to lead the squadron to it and parking on the verge, west side, at about ten yards distant from a dry ditch and shallow hedge cover, up to which the driver and I walked to relieve ourselves. We knew from the radio that Big Mac had set off, so there should not be long to wait. Just time for a cigarette, to feel the warmth of the sun as I unzipped the top half of the khaki flying-suit, and another look at the distant derelict tank through the replacement binoculars I had acquired from the echelon.

During these few minutes an aircraft came in view, a single-seater fighter or fighter-bomber with a radial engine, too high up to read its markings in the bright sunlight. When it circled and lost height, I reckoned it could be a lone Focke-Wulf 190, probably interested in Big Mac's column if that was now out in the open. Yes, there was Mac in the leading wagon just swinging onto the straight past ditched, lamented 95 mm. C Squadron was about to be strafed from the air!

I was wrong. It was our scoutcar that the pilot had spotted, unmistakably at *us* that he put his plane into a dive, from south-east to north-west. The driver and I sprinted for the dry ditch, flung ourselves into its shallow shelter and waited. Up above, the radial engine thrust the dive to a crescendo of sound, above it the whistle of the bomb we were to have all to our two selves.

When the plane had pulled out of its dive and roared up, gaining height to the west, the bomb whistle was still going on. More, it had developed an eccentricity, an unevenness. I forced myself to look up. What the pilot had released was no bomb at all but a jettisoned external petrol capsule, empty and with the airflow making a whistle across an orifice. As I watched, it had ceased to fall straight and was cavorting in circles, like an air-filled balloon released to gyrate and expire.

'All clear!'

As the driver and I moved sheepishly back to the scoutcar, with Big Mac's leading Cromwell only fifty yards from us, I realized that the plane had been no Focke-Wulf but an American Thunderbolt whose pilot did not distinguish friend from foe. The very next evening some of his mates were to dive-bomb a British battalion HQ just before it received a major SS Panzer attack.

At the harbour, Mac said the one word 'Baths' before lolloping over a minor hill in the belief that he would find the colonel on the other side. I asked Jimmy Grimstone whether the rear-link net had disclosed how soon the echelon was likely to reach us. He had heard nothing to suggest it would be before evening. Radio traffic had been brisk, because A and B Squadrons had been virtually cut off for two days, had had several killed and wounded, and a score missing. I could understand that the echelon would need to give them priority attention, which in my view they deserved ahead of Mac's hot baths.

Having myself had a thorough wash and change only the day before, I probably underestimated the discomfort and need of the rest of the squadron. Aloud, within Jimmy's hearing, I remarked that we should probably not see the big petrol cookers before nightfall, so I should go on foot – there being no track for a vehicle to follow – to find the farm-with-a-well marked on the map, and see what squadron baths we could organize there. It was in any case as hot a day as August can produce in latitude 49° N.

I set off across a field of waist-high grass. The scoutcar driver came too, saying he wanted to see a farm. The going proved harder than it looked at first, and what seemed little over a mile from the map felt like five to me by the time we had followed round the perimeter of an orchard to find a way in. After my day of rest at the echelon I had forgotten that I'd spent last night alert and listening for patrols, then this morning stomped the length and breadth of the new harbour to make sure it was safe. Now the absurdity of a flying-suit and boots, so comforting in the watches of the night, for a reconnaissance on foot across uneven fields under the post-noon August sun, made itself felt.

In the orchard was the well. Beyond the well stood the farmhouse, the whole so sheltered from the shimmering heat outside that it felt like Valhalla. There, emerging from the farmhouse, was a solitary Valkyrie, nothing in her attitude to suggest she was anything but alarmed to see us.

'Bonjour, Madame. J'ai cent soldats à baigner' – 'Good day, Madam. I have a hundred soldiers to bath.'

I gestured towards the well. She seemed relieved that that was all we wanted. Nodded: we could use what we liked, plenty of water there.

The scoutcar driver looked at me, could see how tired I was, better than I could. He had left his battledress blouse on the car and been in shirt-sleeve order all the way. Now he volunteered to go back for the squadron and lead them across to the well. If the big petrol cookers had arrived at the harbour, he would see by what means they could hump one over here. But a day like this, who wanted hot water?

I felt I should go back with him, especially if Mac was going to make trouble, which would be for no one but me to face head-on. At the same time, the more I felt my feet tight inside the flying-boots, the less convinced I became about my inclination to make that sweltering journey twice more. The large petrol cookers would probably not have arrived anyway.

So he went alone. The Valkyrie watched him go and went on looking at me. I tried to return her look reassuringly. I wanted to say we would draw the water carefully so as not to pollute the well for drinking-purposes, but the explanation was beyond me. I sat down with my back to the well, still facing her. After another moment she turned and went back into the house. As she closed the door, I fancied I heard a baby cry. I remember wondering if its father might be German. There seemed a great dearth of young Frenchmen hereabout. The peasant in the beret had not been young. If the dad were German, where would he be now, and why had she looked so alarmed at first? Or was it alarm? And then I was asleep.

I was wakened by the first squadron arrivals, swarming over the orchard perimeter with towels, soap and a variety of containers. I moved clear of the well, asking a sergeant to see that people performed their ablutions at some distance from it, likewise that no one was thoughtless enough to pour dirty water back into the well.

I found an apple tree to prop myself against, and set about watching the cooling activity from there. The driver reported there was no sign of the echelon. Major Mac had not returned from RHQ. Most of the squadron would be coming, because it was just the day for a good cold tub, although a few were jibbing at the thought of the walk. He had even brought my wash kit. I thanked him for making the treble journey and he went to strip off and take his turn. I think I dozed some more.

Last to wash, I surveyed the scene from which the rest had now departed, checked the bucket was still working to bring up cool, clear water. I gestured a thank-you towards the farmhouse, too weary to knock and say anything more formally. When I returned to the harbour, the day was already several degrees less hot.

I thought Big Mac would never let up at me for bathing his soldiers in cold water. He returned to the subject next morning, 6 August, when Alastair came from RHQ to visit us, wanting to entertain Charles Pidduck, the general's ADC, to dinner, and to do it at C Squadron rather than at RHQ. Jimmy and I, having both been in the party with Charles and Alastair for that 'meal out' and a visit to the beaches the night before Big Mac returned to the regiment, were all in favour.

Mac consented only with a very bad grace. I was unwise enough to suggest we should ask Tony Venner, who had been on the other party, to come over from A Squadron for the occasion, but Mac vetoed it, beefing about what we were going to feed them all on anyway.

'We could have duckling,' Jimmy suggested brightly.

I felt that might be the turning-point for Mac. He could fancy duckling for himself.

'All right,' he said decisively. 'Ask them – not Tony – and we'll have duckling. Keith messed up the bathing yesterday, so we'll give him the job of organizing the mess for a dinner party and getting hold of the duckling. Jimmy can organize the hot baths for the squadron with the big petrol cookers and show Keith how it should be done.'

Jimmy and I exchanged glances. He had been a second lieutenant when he first knew Mac, which was much longer than I had known him. Now our glance said we would both hold our peace and let the boss get it off his chest or take it out on me, or whatever his odd nature was doing, and certainly we two should not quarrel about it.

Seeing we were accepting his decision, Big Mac made an uncalled-for play upon the surname of Alastair's proposed guest. Alastair departed wondering – as Jim and I did – how Mac would behave that evening. Jimmy went over to the big petrol cookers, and I put my mind to duckling.

The scoutcar driver was quite keen to walk back to the farmhouse and ask if they had duckling going spare, and what they might like in exchange. The mess lance-corporal said he would get a couple of bottles of whatever he could find at the echelon from the regimental mess store. They and anything that had to be bartered for duckling could go on our mess bills. He was quite excited: how pleasant to be in reserve long enough to open the mess and have a dinner party. My assignment was in hand.

During the day some twenty-five pounders arrived and dug in just across the way from us. I talked with the GPO (gun position officer), who said he would soon be punctuating our day when they registered various targets from their changed location. He reckoned his guns would reach some way further forward for the move, which would be useful when the division pushed on again. As I knew, he said, the 11th had been halted by Army order since the 2nd, because its salient was way ahead of neighbours on either flank. Well, I had not known, but I knew now. Perhaps it was the Army order that had called us back from the brink of entering Vire on the 2nd. The GPO seemed to be informed about so much, even that our squadron had not been here long and had just been pulled into reserve after a sharp few days.

Fighter-bombers came and went in ones and twos during the day. They must have seen von Kluge's preparations – or what showed of them – to carry out Hitler's order for an armoured thrust to the west coast, of which we still knew nothing at that time.

It was only on this day, the 6th, that the Americans on our right managed to fight their way into Vire and take it. Armoured units should recognize infantry takes longer. Their move could hardly have pleased Hausser, the SS general commanding the 7th Army, because it took out his most northerly route west. Even so, he had just had use of it for four days longer than he might. If C Squadron had gone on into the town on the night of the 2nd, when it was still lightly held ... Who can say? We might have been wiped out, and yet in war the bold stroke sometimes comes off.

The day became as warm as its predecessor, but C Squadron had hot baths. The evening came and Mac's mood showed no improvement. Alastair arrived with Charles. The mess lance-corporal was in top form. We sat down to duckling with mashed tinned potatoes and a creditable stuffing, together with two bottles of Sauternes that had come with the echelon all the way from Aldershot.

Mac ate heartily, which excused his joining too much in the conversation, but he would mimic Charles's flamboyant mannerisms behind his back, and he seemed not to care if Charles noticed. When the evening light was fading and Alastair as well as Charles seemed relaxed and to be talking freely, I had begun to feel the position retrieved.

Just then we heard aircraft engines and muffled explosions in the distant south-east. Then across the way the GPO sang out a fire order, the numbers one realigned their 'pieces', and a gun barked out its first round. I could not hear what range was called, but all guns were soon firing several rounds for effect. When they paused, we could hear other sounds of firing, and vehicle movement.

Charles rose to his feet, thanked us for a marvellous meal, thought there must be something doing – he had better get back to the general. Alastair excused himself to return to RHQ. Jimmy and I took a walk round the squadron readiness, then I went over to the gun position.

'Sounds like a big attack on the head of our salient,' was the GPO's verdict. 'I suspect they're probing round the flanks as well.'

'Like probing up to here?'

'Oh, we shall nail them long before they get this far. Can't let them get to the gun line, y'know.'

We knew nothing at all about what the enemy was at, not even Charles. The reality was that the Panzer assault on the American lines was scheduled to begin at midnight, but 10th SS was launching its practised fury upon British 11th Armoured a few hours early. The help the enemy got before dark from the American Thunderbolts must have surprised those of his troops who saw it. The Brits dug in on the Perrier ridge, and their supporting Shermans, probably reckoning they were in for a long night anyway. They called for defensive fire on the enemy's known forming-up areas, and got it in good measure from their own gunners and also neighbouring American batteries.

C Squadron set guards, and I made myself go to bed, where I actually slept for much of the night, mostly for an hour or more at a time. Each time I roused, the guns were still firing, pausing only while a fresh range was called. In my drowsy state I thought the range called each time was lower than its predecessor.

Beyond the small hours I crawled out, wrapped up against the chill, and walked over to the gun position. My cheerful friend looked up from his calculations, received his mug of tea and a spare one for me, acknowledged what had just come through his headphones and called a new range to a shadowy figure lurking nearby, who passed it on to the gun crews.

'You knew when to come.' I thought at first he meant the tea. 'First time we've increased the range for several hours. Must have turned them at last ... Just as well, ammunition running low, barrels red hot, quite a night!'

The sipped tea coursed through me. 10th SS, who had brought the Red Army's central winter offensive to a halt, had now themselves been turned. Further south, although we should not hear of it yet, their fellow Panzer formations were about to be checked by an American defence that proved as dogged as our own. Once daylight allowed a resumption of flying, the ordered counter-offensive would peter out altogether.

9 Final Eleven

Hitler blamed von Kluge for the counter-offensive failure, contending he had attacked before all the Panzers were ready. 'Clever Hans' and his immediate subordinates knew better. If they had waited even one more day, they would have missed the last chance to carry out the Führer's order. As it was, from 7 August the Allies had too many formations for the number of roads available, all closing in upon a tightening circle – a circle except for one sector of escape towards the Seine – in which a still fierce 5th Panzer Army and the remnants of Hausser's torn and battered 7th Army were determined to fight every yard of the way.

Our division was to change sectors with the Guards Armoured. So we were to occupy a tight patch vacated by that Scottish Division we had first worked with in June. They in turn were moving east of Caen ready for a general push to the Seine. The juggling gave our regiment the prospect of a move, and some time off as well.

On the 9th I was allowed to take a lorry-load of enthusiasts to a local river to swim. We plunged through the weeds to the deeper part of some strangely unbuoyant water and cooled ourselves idly from the day's heat. Returning to the squadron, there was the lance-corporal I had put with his agitated appendix into the ambulance at the end of July, now sent back not operated on but labelled 'false alarm'. He must have noticed some changes in the composition of the squadron.

The 9th was the day when 12th SS, our division's earliest antagonists in Normandy, having some Tiger

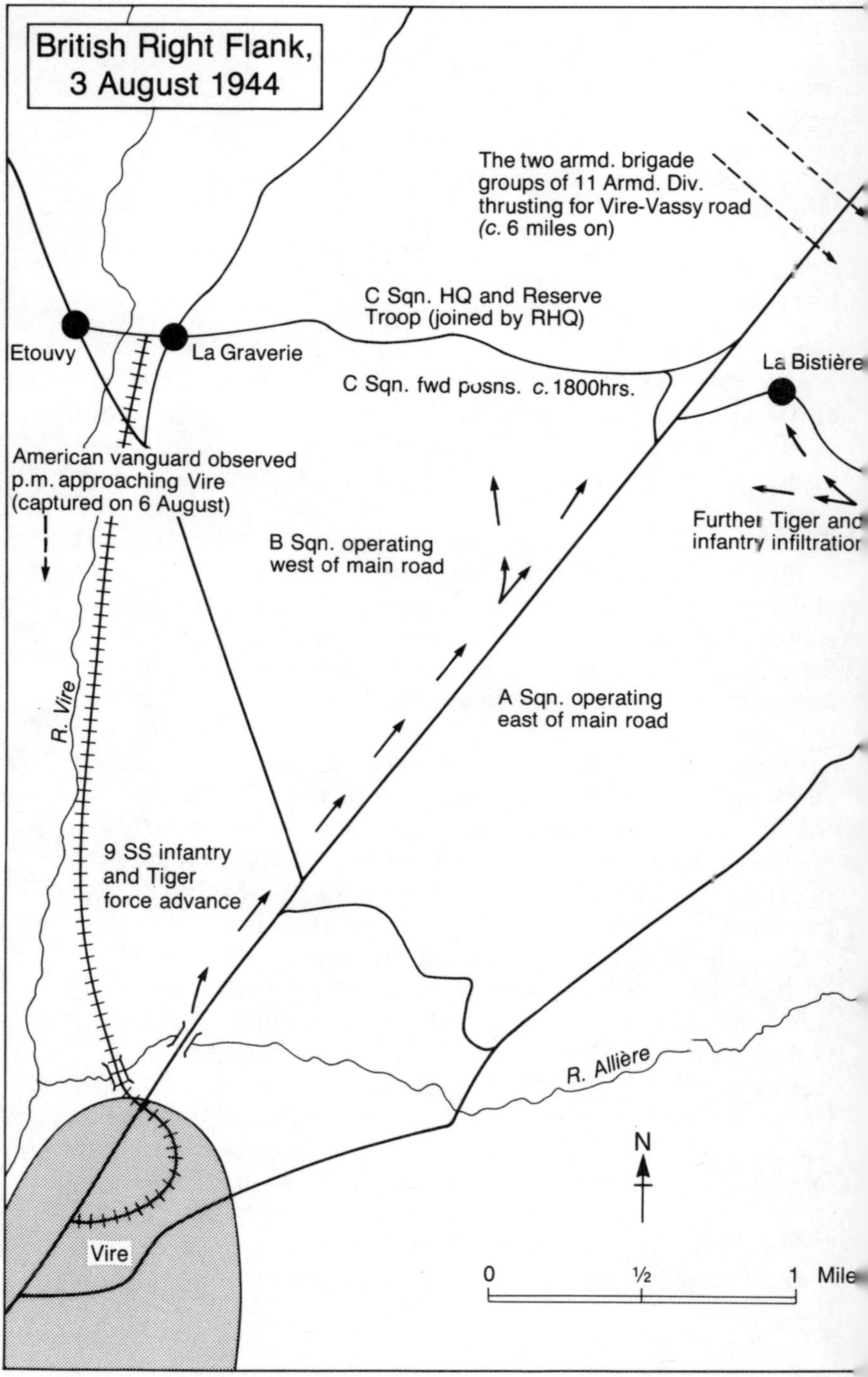
British Right Flank,
3 August 1944
The two armd. brigade groups of 11 Armd. Div. thrusting for Vire-Vassy road (c. 6 miles on)
C Sqn. HQ and Reserve Troop (joined by RHQ)
Etouvy
La Graverie
La Bistière
C Sqn. fwd posns. c. 1800hrs.
American vanguard observed p.m. approaching Vire (captured on 6 August)
Further Tiger and infantry infiltration
B Sqn. operating west of main road
R. Vire
A Sqn. operating east of main road
9 SS infantry and Tiger force advance
R. Allière
N
Vire
0
½
1 Mile

tanks and other 88 mm guns at their disposal, persistently counter-attacked the Canadian advance south of Caen, so that one armoured regiment lost at least forty-five of its Shermans in an afternoon. They had only landed about ten days previously.

When the regiment moved, Tony Venner and I set off together in scoutcars to prepare the new harbour areas for our respective squadrons. Going by the shortest route from the map, I was in the lead as we mounted a hill into closely wooded country. For some reason I shall never explain in logic, I suddenly knew we were into an ambush. I U-turned my driver where the hard shoulder widened, waving to Tony to stick close and get down in the car. We had retreated ten yards before machine-gun fire rattled off both rear engine plates, stick and egg grenades fell all round, and bombs from a small mortar pursued our departure to a greater range. Then I looked at the map for a longer way round.

Lieutenant-General Horrocks visited us to shake the hand of every officer and welcome us to 30 Corps, to which we should be transferred on the 14th. Recovering from wounds sustained in North Africa, he was newly arrived from Britain to take corps command. He outlined how we should spearhead the pursuit of a retreating enemy.

On the morning of the 14th we set off from the Estry area in the general direction of Vassy, the regiment leading the infantry brigade group, A Squadron left, C right, off and on carrying an infantry company on the tank engine covers. Through delightful treed country the narrow tracks and roads wind their ways downhill and up again, crossing and recrossing murmuring streams that sometimes disappear into culverts, soon to re-emerge. The whole scene is for ever a military engineer's joy, for the opportunities it affords to blow up key bridges, conceal mines and booby-traps, fell trees where they will best obstruct, hide an anti-tank gun to cover an obstacle, or a machine-gun to wait until you get out to remove a mine.

By nine in the evening A Squadron had lost its scoutcar

on a mined bridge, and a tank to an anti-tank gun. A and B Squadrons then supported an infantry attack onto a high ridge near Vassy.

The 15th was a day of less progress in cautious reconnaissance. C Squadron harboured early, circling gratefully into an open field. Before the column came to a halt, Big Mac gave the order to clear guns. A sergeant who had just quit his cramped turret to relax in front of it was drilled in the back by a round from his own Besa. The wound was close to the spine. We tried to make our comrade more comfortable as he breathed shallowly and developed a cold sweat. When the MO arrived, he borrowed a pin to jab at the casualty's heel and ask if he felt anything. Paralysis below the waist was the solemn verdict. As the ambulance went off, we all hoped the condition might prove only temporary. The victim was evacuated, and we heard no more at the time, but he died the next day.

The regiment went into divisional reserve for the 16th, the infantry brigade group moving towards Flers, the armoured group in the direction of Condé. A and B Squadrons went in the evening to clear an area north of Flers, losing a tank and a scoutcar, but it was on the morning of the 17th that C Squadron took the lead again, carrying an infantry company, to enter the town of Flers, from which the enemy had withdrawn.

The welcome of the populace brought us to a standstill. A young and attractive blonde woman, described as secretary to the town resistance leader, called up to me that she was instructed to speak with a certain Captain Field. Probably only two of us in the regiment knew that name, that it belonged to the divisional field security officer. I flicked to regimental net and called Alastair, using the day's code card for FSO, to explain who was being sought. Alastair called division on his rear link, and came back at once to say Captain Field was on his way by jeep to this very market-place, where he would now be watching out for an unmistakable young woman with very fair hair. I jumped down from the tank to convey this message without shouting, and was rewarded by a spanking hug and kiss, to roars of approval from troops and the crowd.

Big Mac reacted also: 'Driver, advance! What is Captain Jones at now?'

On the road to Briouze we experienced occasional opposition and some delay from mines, but even more from the many unarmed enemy who wanted to be taken prisoner. Mostly we pointed back towards the town, for them to surrender to someone, anyone but us. When we were halted anyway, I looked in a few paybooks and asked the odd question to see if a pattern would emerge of the formations in front of us. It was impossible: the variety of unit identifications reflected the chaos of stragglers left behind by the organized escape plan.

I addressed in German one swarthy corporal wearing a very clean uniform of the 2nd SS Panzer Division, the armband neatly bearing its name, 'Das Reich'. The division had been left point of the abortive Mortain counter-thrust ten days before, but where was it now? (Actually, von Kluge had extricated it and 9th SS to refit at Vimoutiers outside the 'pocket', and to counter-attack from outside when our Polish Armoured Division closed the gap during the next very few days.) The man answered my questions in English with an accent suggesting he had learned from Americans. He had lost his paybook. He was Hungarian, he said, and a chef. When he woke that morning, his unit was gone. He had bathed and scented himself and put on this uniform, ready to greet the Americans or the British. I pointed rearwards, and we moved on.

By midday we were nearly four miles beyond Flers. By evening, felled trees and spasmodic gunfire still impeded our approach to Briouze. A and B Squadrons had been deployed to left and right but the main goal remained elusive. Harbouring about 10 p.m. in the dark off the main road, we were told some news that had shattering impact: we had fought our last day as a regiment. A full-strength cavalry unit had arrived which would take our place in the morning.

The mail was brought – for me a letter in a hand I did not recognize. I stuffed it into my pocket unread. There was so much to do before bed, as we were to be off on transporters in the morning, back to the beaches' tank-park. From there nearly 200 of us would go at once as reinforcements to the four armoured regiments of the 7th Armoured Division, which was already all Cromwell tanks except for its one-in-four Fireflies. There we should become Desert Rats, European version.

The thought seemed to comfort no one. There perhaps, from those who had been at it all the war, we should learn some real soldiering. There, some of us would experience, at the sharpest end, an insidious sense of fear. But here in Normandy, it was our sixty-fourth day since landing.

Regimental statistics would come later: eighty-seven killed, some seventy wounded and forty-six missing, altogether two-thirds of normal tank-crew strength. The officer content: fourteen dead, the same number wounded, six missing. Reinforcement was not available on such scale. This was to be the general problem now of the British Liberation Army, even more acute in the infantry. Whereas fresh troops would continue to arrive across the Atlantic to replace United States casualties and augment the total number of their formations, Britain had reached the limit. Montgomery could only disband a selection of his depleted units and divisions to render others viable. Some of us were about to experience that process.

By March 1945 and the Rhine crossing, United States forces would outnumber British and Canadian by three to one. Yet here in Normandy, the British and Canadian effort had been paramount, deliberately drawing enemy armour away from the Americans. The Panzer divisions from the beginning became committed to front-line defence and to plugging gaps, so that they could not be gathered for an effective counter-thrust. Constant attacks around Caen convinced the enemy of a threat to Paris from the eastern end of the beachhead, enabling the build-up of US divisions to break out and cross France with minimal opposition. No American armoured division landed until 2 July, and none was committed in action before the 26th.

On our sixty-fourth day, the Battle of Normandy had been all but won. Montgomery, commanding all US and British land forces, had compressed the enemy into a shrinking net. Through the 'Falaise Gap', escaping soldiery would run the gauntlet of Allied air punishment for five more days. Unencumbered by a part in closing the gap, the American 3rd Army could press on virtually unopposed for Paris and the Seine. Orders would send an American corps along the south bank towards the sea, to cut off the enemy's line of retreat to the river, to achieve a 'double envelopment'. After initial progress the corps was halted by opposition near Elbeuf, mission half-accomplished. British and Canadian formations would have to fight the practised rearguards of the 5th Panzer Army all the way to the river west of Rouen, while many German survivors and some hundred armoured vehicles were got across the Seine despite the absence of intact bridges.

On the day of our disbandment Field Marshal Model – 'Hitler's Fireman' – arrived to take over from von Kluge, who was to report to Berlin, on suspicion of treachery. 'Clever Hans' took poison on the way back. Model was to keep going until the following year, when, surrounded in the Ruhr, he shot himself.

In the tank-park overlooking the Channel I was approached by Bill, now a lance-sergeant, Albert, Harry and Stan. They had been sounding out one or two people, they said, and if I would back them up, they thought they could work it that we got back together as a crew, in their old rear-link tank. I conferred with their present officer, respectfully with my 95 mm ex-C Squadron crew and with OC Tank-Park. All agreed. I moved my kit, and we were ready to become five Desert Rats together. The exchange of crew made no difference to the fact that every officer who was to go to 7th Armoured had already been allocated to a unit, in my case the premier regiment of the 'black berets'.

Who else of my acquaintance, apart from my original crew, would now be moving where? Jimmy Grimstone would join a Royal Tanks unit in the same brigade, Alastair Hetherington was booked for 11th Armoured Div. HQ. Bobby Lorimer, the adjutant, had the winding-up of the yeomanry to complete and would then go initially to an Army Group training regiment. Edward Fletcher, Ernie Ehrenfeld and Tim Peck were dead. Big Mac – the canny one – was destined for a cavalry unit. With him would go Tony Venner and most other ranks in the old C Squadron, the survivors from those with whom they had spent the largest part of the war. Lord George Scott, the second-in-command, was to be CO of a sister yeomanry regiment, with him a few of the originals, hopefully including Lance-Corporal Nobby Clark, although I have been unable to establish this for certain. The colonel himself, a regular cavalry officer no longer young, was understood to be returning to Britain to a training command.

Mail from my beloved had reached the park. I wrote to her giving our next expected official address. Then I thought of the letter I had not opened the night before. It was from the second lieutenant whose ear had been bleeding after the stonk near La Bistière. I read it now, addressed from a hospital in Scotland. Latterly it enquired about his lost kit, so that I sent an immediate signal to Bobby the adjutant, but the opening lines I quote verbatim:

> Dear Keith, You are the only person I know for sure to be alive in the Squadron. Also I have to thank you for getting me out of all the confusion. I have no recollection of what happened from the time I had the scoutcar in a corner of the field with some baled out crews, except for an impression of seeing my mapboard shatter. I also remember walking across country some distance until I

was put on a jeep and driven to some Aid Post. I understand my ear suffered internal damage and it will be quite some time before …

Yours very sincerely,
Gus Howes

PS Lieut. Bromhead (Blue) is here.

ABBREVIATIONS

ACV	Armoured command vehicle, a bullet-proof 'office' on wheels for staff officers at a Main HQ.
ADC	Aide-de-camp, a general's personal assistant.
AP	Armour-piercing shot (distinguished from high explosive shell).
CO	Commanding officer.
GSO 3 (or G3)	General staff officer, grade 3 (a captain).
HE	High explosive.
IO	Intelligence officer, primarily concerned with information about the enemy.
LO	Liaison officer, available to travel to and maintain links between units or formations working together.
LST	Landing ship, tank. Capable of transporting at least a squadron of tanks inside, with the scoutcars and half-tracks of RHQ on deck.
MG	Machine gun: Besa in a Cromwell, Browning in a Sherman.
MO	Medical Officer.
OP	Observation post, spotting for artillery; often a major mounted in a tank.
RHQ	Regimental headquarters.
RV	Rendezvous, meeting point.

Index